GW00871573

Continually i̱ ̟ ̱ ̱ .

Also by Jane Burdiak

Patchwork

Domestic Science

Between the Stars

THE WALK

To Simon
Best wishes
Jane Burdiak.

For Isaac

Jane Burdiak

THE WALK

AUSTIN MACAULEY
PUBLISHERS LTD.

A CIP catalogue record for this title is available from the British
Library.

ISBN 978 184963 745 9

www.austinmacauley.com

First Published (2014)
Austin Macauley Publishers Ltd.
25 Canada Square
Canary Wharf
London
E14 5LB

Printed and bound in Great Britain

1

Effortlessly, the first week of the rest of her life had slipped passed.

It had not seemed a week since her last day, rigorous as ever and busy until the bitter end. She wouldn't miss that lesson, last thing on a Friday afternoon, a single lesson of six girls, quiet studious girls, and fourteen boys, more than half of whom were garrulous, very rowdy, and persistently disruptive, however planned the lesson was. The lesson left her skin feeling clammy and her face flushed. Inside, her anxious heart was beating harder. Three thirty could not come soon enough, but the large hand of the clock barely moved. Throughout the fifty minutes there was chatter and clatter, missiles were thrown, plastic bottles crushed, crayons launched, water spilt, stools scraped. I-pods and phones rang and messages were sent. Eyes were averted to screens out of sight below the tables, but from her strategic position across the room she could see them plainly. The epidemic of these devices in the last twelve years had become obsessive. They were a scourge. She didn't blame them. But why could they not be more discrete? When asked what discrete meant, their faces looked puzzled. They saw no point at all in writing and making notes and no point in listening to her wittering on about sustainability. What did they care? They were only interested in getting out at three thirty. She remembered a similar Friday afternoon about fourteen years ago, pre-dating Blackberry handsets, it was when blackberries were fruits and picked in late summer, bursting with juice, bleeding and staining – not the convenient little hand-held screen that opened up the world.

Two weeks ago, when she last saw them she decided not to give them her attention, preferring instead to ignore them and sit perched on a stool, observing, writing in her A4 planner. The work, she wrote on the board, there was no need to speak. Slowly the big hand edged towards the four. Ten minutes to go. Knowing that the group would be her very last lesson ever, she would have to keep a tight sail. They had got wind of her year ten groups being lavished with personalised fairy cakes and wondered if they were going to have them too. She didn't think so, giving the excuse of it being the last day of term. All week she dreaded and fretted about the lesson and its content, and even though she preferred a formal lesson as opposed to a 'fun' one, it would have to be something a bit different for her to get her teeth into if nothing else. Reluctantly and painstakingly and not without love she personalized twenty iced fairy cakes in red lettering which she gave to them on leaving the room. She also made twenty pizza swirls which she served while evaluating their decorated cake ideas and introduced them to product analysis. She encouraged them to write copious amounts on the outer wrapper of Starburst chewy sweets, followed by the individual sweet wrapper, and then finally the sensory qualities of the sweet itself. Some were staggered by the amount that they wrote. After all, it was only a small chewy sweet.

After giving Gina and Gina from Tom's harem of cleaning ladies big hugs she was ready to leave, somehow she would miss those women from Ghana, their dependable resilience, their flashing smiles, and the patriotic love that they had for each other.

She had enjoyed being a teacher. A demanding occupation, but it had allowed her to grow in every way and yet still be herself. It was like going on the stage every day, applying make-up, putting on a costume and learning the lines. She thought she could do it twenty years ago when her own children were still children and needed her hand to cross the road. The decision to apply to a local college to do her PGCE had been difficult but once started it became how it was. It had been hard work, but never dull and never boring.

Had she been single she could see that like others she would have made teaching her life, totally immersing herself in the vocation, carving a career, investing in the students. But there were other things in which to plough her energy.

She relied on the pupil's enjoyment of the lesson to diffuse any potential problems of poor behaviour and liked to think that the pupils would remember their lessons with her Maybe when they were much older they would remember the 'wicked' bolognaise or the 'cool' minestrone soup or how to use their hands and brain simultaneously; discover the cold-wet slipperiness of raw chicken, alert their senses to the pungent aroma of cumin – cumin because it had a smell of body odour – how to manipulate a peeler around a potato or be dexterous with a can opener. She would never know if they remembered.

In between lessons on that last day colleagues and pupils came to say goodbye. With them they brought flowers and cards and chocolates, along with hugs and kisses. Her goodbye 'do' had been on Wednesday at lunch time. Fish and chips had been ordered and champagne served. She received special presents and cards strewn with signatures wishing her luck in her retirement. Swiping out for the last time she did not feel sad or even nostalgic when she handed Val in reception her keys. It was final. There was no going back. The 'new' teacher, her replacement, was already installed. And no, she was not coming back as a supply teacher nor was she going to do exam invigilation, she was going to go and do all the things that she had not had time for over the last twenty years. She was going to dance.

Looking back, it had been a good week but how quickly memories faded into obscurity. She had made no plans and the pressure was off. With retirement came a carefree relaxation that she had forgotten existed and it surprised her how quickly she settled into the new rhythm of the day. She would not miss that feeling of dread on a Sunday evening or the prospect of some classes scattered throughout the week. She would not miss packing up her 'bag for life' or maybe two bags with ingredients for shepherd's pie or/and a gingerbread or slipping on an apple peel carelessly dropped, flailing and spinning round, grabbing for stability before being impaled across a cooker, or apologizing for the lingering smell of onions or curry when she went to the hairdressers or the dentist after school, or food glued to her shoes or throbbing legs and distended veins from standing all day and feet that expanded at least a size by lunch time, or her waistband wet from the trickling sweat of ten ovens firing at 200 degrees...and the marking, the never ending marking. The holidays, especially the long summer holidays, begrudged by some and envied by others were what had kept her going, recharging the batteries, but after two weeks the feeling of looming apprehension as she approached half way and the rapid slide to the end of August chewed and gnawed with trepidation. She would not miss waking up to see the road drowning in snow and driving the eight miles to school on high alert, rigid in her seat, tense with concentration.

After being 'warmer than average for the time of year' for two weeks, warm enough to re-install the table and chairs in the garden, it turned more seasonal. In a word, it turned cold. Like pale shell coloured snow, petals spiralled like confetti to the ground in the biting wind. It no longer mattered that the sharp blue sky was shrouded in a thickening glaucoma of cloud, nor did it matter that on the very first day of the rest of her life she felt hung over. Time was her own to do with as she wanted.

Had she felt good she would have been in the pool, making the most of the nine o'clock start, as it was she felt delicate and still a little confused with drink. She did not contribute her fragile feeling entirely to the very pleasant evening with her family in their local pub, more to the lack of sleep on the Thursday night, the very exacting Friday, being guilty of becoming dehydrated and not stopping for lunch and no-one checking that she had eaten.

She lay listening to the night; drifting in and out of sleep. In the early hours muffled voices and distant steps came into focus. As they neared she could hear them talking and listened without hearing what they said. Gradually their footsteps trailed away, their voices dissolved in the still black night. With the vague light came squawking crows and a community warblers, then she was aware of the bolt vibrating in the wall twenty feet below her pillow. Next-door-but-one's cat having finished prowling for the night had leapt to the top of the back gate to drop silently and slink home behind the hedge to lie curled contentedly in a sunny square. Except for the edges, the big fat pillow beneath her restless head was hard. The feathers had become compacted and it was too warm from the heat of her head. It needed a good shake and an airing. In her left eye there was a persistent vortex of grey shapes that disappeared into a hole.

Hearing the ping of the clock when it reached quarter to six, still programmed to launch her into her day, she was glad that there were no demands. Behind closed eyelids tadpoles hung upside down alternating with pieces of coloured glass – she assumed them to be coloured, but are dreams coloured? – that fell into changing patterns like a kaleidoscope. Prisms of crazy-paving occupied the periphery. At one stage she got up and went downstairs. It was all in order, as she had left it the previous evening apart from the two cups of coffee sat in places at the table waiting to be drunk. Compelled, she dipped her little finger into one. It was cold, stone cold. Methodically she emptied them down the drain and placed them in the dishwasher. That was enough activity and she made her way back to the drowsy warmth of bed. Outside, the day had started. In between the sounds of cars that had a total disregard for the speed limit and travelling far too fast despite the radical traffic calming measures, birds sang cheery arias on the telephone line outside the bedroom window.

By eleven, after a cup of tea and two Paracetamols administered by her husband she found herself unloading the fridge of sausages, bacon and eggs and making the 'all important' breakfast for her two flagging sons who were also in a state of disrepair and her husband who saw their company as an excuse to indulge.

The next day however, with her energy restored, her Sunday morning routine resumed, making a batch of Chelsea Buns and drop-scones before slipping into the pool at nine. Being the start of the school holidays the usual schedule was abandoned and the public swim brought forward, resulting in a fairly empty pool that allowed her to swim up and down without interruption. The afternoon was occupied making dinner for everyone which meant that she did not venture far from the kitchen.

Occasionally she thought sod it, or to hell with it and lashed out extravagantly and impulsively on sirloin steak or smoked salmon or asparagus or ready-grated cheese, little luxuries that she could ill-afford, but for whatever reason, a birthday or a special meal, it was justified. She went shopping with a list and rarely wavered from it. Generally, she had always been careful and not succumbed to tempting offers like buy one get one free grated cheese, bought for, but not used in the pizza swirls on the last day of term. To keep it free-flowing and prevent it congealing at the bottom of the bag, each strand of cheese was coated in a thin layer of potato starch, rendering it practically useless for most culinary purposes. On top of scones it cooked to a golden crisp and inside it melted into a labyrinth of waxy tunnels. It didn't resemble freshly grated cheese at all and however tempting the offer, she would not be buying it again. When she perused the shelves or the chill cabinets or the freezers she was always acutely aware of weight or the size or the cost and the value. For instance it was cheaper to buy two separate bars of soap than a twin pack.

She started a list. She called it a thrift list and on it she recorded any time that she had opened her purse and spent some money. It lasted only a few days. She recalled writing such lists when she was first married, writing neatly in pounds, shillings and pence.

Having more time to prepare it, food became more inventive. She would nosey in the fridge and the cupboards looking for inspiration. Everything seemed less trouble.

As long as she had an onion she reckoned that she could practically make food out of thin air. Indeed, most of the time the fridge was full of cold thin air. She cut her coat according to her cloth and was forever substituting one ingredient for another, run out of flour – add some oats – that was her motto. She would fry an onion and odds and ends and make a slurry with half a can of tomatoes and a sprinkling of herbs then combine it with some cooked pasta. The most economical meal had to be liver and onions, 44p plus peas and new potatoes from the garden and a sad cabbage wilting in the fridge. Dealing with the slippery tissue, liver always reminded her of the leather inner-sole-casserole served up at her Aunt Dorothy's when, in black and white, Dixon of Dock Green said 'Good evening all' on television on a Saturday evening. Eating it in this way was a lasting memory, mumping and mumping until it was grey and there was no taste left, then, apart from feeding it to the cat, wondering how to dispose of the sinewy lump filling her mouth without being seen. Remembering too on her first day of having school dinners at secondary school, she chewed and chewed at a gristly lump and in the end had to fain blowing her nose, discretely off-loading it into her hanky.

Bizarrely, there were some foods of little nutritional value and concocted of God knows what, that could not be compromised, like the golden crumbs used to coat fish fingers and available in tubs which she used regularly when making Scotch eggs, preferring the dazzling orange colour to dull wholemeal crumbs or her own home made. She liked gloopy cherry pie filling and the congealed solidness of a greasy pork pie. Nor did she have an aversion to the odd handy little jar of curry paste. Other than that her cupboards contained basic ingredients, staples like beans, flour, pasta, rice and tinned tomatoes.

She really liked white bread, but rarely ate it, finding that it adhered to her teeth, and she imagined bite-size dumplings of dough feeding their way through her intestines. Recently, she had taken to mushy peas, first tried in Borough Market, where it was trendy and now served up and down the land in miniscule dishes on the plate. Why had she always opted for bright green peas? As she said, buying sirloin steak was a luxury as was a leg of lamb. Gradually the cost had become prohibitive. But how she loved them, eating them completely on their own, no amount would satisfy her lust. In the same breath she could become a vegetarian and live on grains and beans, fruit and vegetables. The taste of fruit however was unpredictable. Most lacked flavour and tasted of nothing in particular, eaten for medicinal reasons rather than the taste. Strawberries on their own were tasteless, watery and bland, however, serve them in a heavenly meringue nest with a good dollop of cream and the taste is transformed. Vegetables were more versatile and didn't require sugar to make them palatable. When she worked, fruit was her mainstay for lunch but now retired she doubted that she lived up to the five-a-day recommendation.

Her incapacity to get to the Post Office and Health Centre on Saturday morning prompted an early start on Monday. As it was achieved she struck her pen through each job on her list. After dropping her son off at the station, she had time until her hospital appointment at one to call in at Laura Ashley and look at the wallpapers and their tempting reductions in the spring sale. Of course the one she really wanted, a matt white paper hanging with lilac fronds, was not in the sale. She selected two papers and took them to the assistant who tore off a sample length of each.

The follow-up appointment with the neurosurgeon had been activated with an automated phone call the previous Thursday. She was far-from-pleased at the thought of spending any time at the hospital. It was to be the last of a series of appointments since November when all of a sudden her joys and expectations had come to an abrupt end.

She had felt a strange unexplainable feeling. Gripping hold of normality she tried to realize the sensation of each step, her shoe on the ground, her foot in her shoe, her toes in her sock. She wasn't ready to be taken away, to be hospitalised or detained. She needed pyjamas and a new sponge bag. Her legs needed waxing and her eyebrows tinting. She needed to leave a list of instructions on the kitchen table on how to operate the washing machine for different loads. She hadn't written a will. It came to her that the disturbance that she felt was like she had when on a three week course of steroids, prescribed at the time to control the hideous pain until surgery could be done. The experience was a strange sensation, a light-headedness like a draught or aura, a feeling that rolled in and out like a wave. She tried to stay in control, to focus. Conscious of being able to observe, she watched herself coping with the strange floating sensation, dealing with her balance and the blur. Making simple mistakes when writing she was constantly shaking her head to concentrate. On the surface she came over as being completely calm but inside impulses coursed through her, pulsating like an electric current, ready to blow a fuse at any moment. Nothing was left undone, nothing left to chance. Like a chameleon she was gradually changing into her mother. Indeed the mirror was increasingly reflecting her stoop and the set of her mouth, her mannerisms, but other characteristics were beginning to show.

The episode on the plane, the seizure, had left her feeling grey and elderly and instead of coming home from the wonderful holiday fit and refreshed she was frightened and exhausted. Remembering little of the incident she asked her husband to tell her. He of course was reluctant to and tended to ignore it, not thinking or wanting to think that it was any more than a bad dream. In her mind words like fit or epileptic fit, seizure, paroxysm or abnormal disorder conjured an image unimaginable, of mad-houses, institutions, mental homes, workhouses, it was terrifying. Feeling as though everything was going to end, she had to be ready. So this was what people did when they reached sixty, she thought as she waited for her name to be called over the Tannoy, because they were mainly over sixty. They were in various stages of sixty and in various shapes of health and in various shapes. Limps exaggerated, slowness dramatized, coughs, and things that could not be seen. She did not want to be there. Having already been for the all-important tests she was at the surgery again waiting for the results. What were the findings going to show? Her name was called. She walked along the corridor and turned right. She knocked and walked in. She took a seat. "How can I help?" asked the doctor. Briefly she related the story. After a moment the doctor remembered the telephone call nearly three weeks earlier when she had recommended that she didn't drive. Since then she had complained bitterly about the frustration and inconvenience of not being allowed to drive. All the tests had come back normal. That was good but led to the next step of making an appointment with the neurologist. It could be weeks. Until then she hadn't felt old, she planned to live until ninety at least, however, it was obvious to others that she was because she was handed innovative skin care products in Selfridges and offered a seat on the underground. There must be signs. She became uncharacteristically aggressive, ruthlessly busy, constantly occupied. Things had to be done urgently. She pushed herself to the limit. She resented being a burden on others, organising lifts with people. Having her independence withdrawn was unbearable. Then, on top of that, she had a fall.

She knew all about the stairs. They were eighty years old and spoke in creaks and moans. She had known them for half that time and could take them two at a time, or singly when carrying tea, lugging furniture, or carrying her sleeping babies. She and her children knew where to tread lightly to avoid being heard. Even in the dark she knew them like the back of her hand, which was obviously not well enough. Thinking that she was already at the bottom, she stepped and lost her balance. Unable to regain it she spiralled out of control towards the front door. Half turning, her back caught the brick pier. Her ribs cracked like a whip. Breathless and whimpering she fell to the floor, winded and wounded. The knotted fist of pain under her ribs made her feel faint. Folded in a crouched position she could barely breathe, imagining shards of sheared bone and blackened blood. She remembered getting ready for school. Opening her eyes she looked through the laths of her fingers. Bright gelatinous eyes of blood slipped from her throat and over her tongue and into the sink of water, darkening it a rusty brown colour. It was the smell of old rusting baking tins. She pulled the plug. The combination of these things could be seen as being related. She said nothing. Gradually her bones mended. In the end, however, her appointment amounted to no more than a clean bill of health. She expected nothing less and shook the Consultant's extended hand and said goodbye. The awful intrusion was over.

It was the perfect day. Her husband left her hanging the freshly ironed shirts and blouses in the wardrobe. From there she gathered-up the washing and put it on. Then she transported Mr Henry upstairs and chugged around. Her son had recently moved out and in his wake was a trail of debris. There was only one place for it, a pink sack. Into the now empty wardrobe she put all her son's artwork that had leaned against the bedroom wall for years. She rediscovered the carpet. She loved messing about on her hands and knees in the garden with her thumb and forefinger prising chickweed and speedwell from the gravel, getting the entire root, going for a swim, going to the dump to offload the accumulated rubbish, walking into town to post a letter, choosing a book in the library, getting caught in the rain.

Removing the old grout in the bathroom gave complete satisfaction. She could feel the saliva filling the corner of her mouth as she concentrated, again her thumb and forefinger applying pressure, feeling pleased when it came away cleanly. Disposing of the gritty mess covering the bath she vacuumed and opened the window, leaving the air to dry it thoroughly before her husband re-grouting the next day.

It never ceased to amaze her that so much could be done within twenty four hours, one minute she was walking in Dimmingsdale woods in Staffordshire with her husband and their dear friends and their dog Ted and the next she was boarding the train to London with her son.

They caught the train at 1.40pm. It seemed late in the day. To her – not to make the most of the day seemed wasteful. From South Kensington they walked to Blackett Laboratory in Prince Consort Road. The 'pedestrian friendly' road layout where Cromwell Road and Exhibition Road met was a vast improvement, completely diluting the heaving congestion that normally funnelled between the Natural History Museum and the Science Museum especially during the holidays. Collecting her son in reception, they went to The Queen's Arms for a late lunch before, especially for his brother's benefit, having a guided tour of his lab. Whenever she had gone it seemed an Aladdin's cave of organised chaos, overseen by up-coming mad scientists. The afternoon soon dissolved and it was time to return to Euston to catch the 253 bus to Hackney to view her son's Framed Work exhibited in Biddle Bros. Being peak time the bus stopped at every stop weaving its way slowly through Camden Town, as always, awash with people, Finsbury Park, Stamford Hill and into Hackney. From her front row seat on the top deck she settled to take in the sights, every continent was represented, every tribe and ethnic culture, every social class was there, from the affluent to the impoverished and the destitute. She had seen her son's work on its opening night at the beginning of March and thought it important that his brother, who at the time was unable to come, also saw it. And so it was arranged. It was the first time she had gone out for the day with her eldest son and she had wondered how it would be. It was good.

Besides her husband and herself, unhurried thin legged spiders lived in their house too. Their flimsy webs reached between ornaments or across pan handles or between the tub of cocoa and the packet of lasagne or draped from ceiling corners to hinges. Unchecked, she could see that they could take hold at an alarming rate, weaving a delicate net over everything, their home quickly looking like Miss Havisham's house in Great Expectations.

The following week she emptied two kitchen drawers of all their paraphernalia, throwing away the accumulated rubbish, pastry brushes that shed their bristles on the mince pies, defunct plungers of cafetieres, curly plastic straws, wooden forks and plastic spoons – kept because they could be useful – but never used. She vacuumed the build-up of crumbs and dust and relined them with fresh wallpaper. She washed the compartment trays and restored law and order to the cutlery. They must have had a bit of a tidy three years ago but at breakfast she asked her husband when he last went to France. It was 2003 when she last emptied the drawers. Next came what was known as the cereal cupboard as it used to be when her children lived at home where the breakfast cereals were kept. Now it housed tins, tins of tomatoes, and beans, cannellini, flageolet, kidney, mixed and of course baked. There were also other tins, bought for certain recipes waiting patiently for their turn to be used. She was pleased that they were all in date. Lurking at the back however were two boxes of breadsticks bought with dips in mind, one was completely sealed dated 2011 and the other one, its perforated seal broken but with two sealed sachets remaining, was dated 2008.

It was her birthday. Lying awake during the night she thought about her mother and how it had been on 16th April 1951 when she was born, confined as she had been in The Haven, a mother and baby home, spring sunshine flooding over the scrubbed floorboards, windows latched open, curtains murmuring in a draught of warm April air. At last she slept again, sleeping passed the ping of the clock. She thought how her day ahead would have been, hanging her clothes ready the night before, covering the windscreen of the car to protect against the predicted frost, putting the bins out, making breakfast, gathering her things together and driving to work, swiping in and getting ready for the day. In her head, she could picture the day and what would happen, pupils lining-up, registration, their faces and how they would react, resisting, reluctant and understandably hostile but gradually by the end of the lesson they would come to accept the change and realize that the 'new' lady was much the same as the 'old' one.

Being her birthday absorbed her day. There were cards and presents and phone calls and her husband took her for lunch. She remembered last year's champagne birthday, being woken with a cup of tea. That in itself was unusual. Something was going on and suddenly, by seven everyone was up and about getting dressed in nothing very important. What was going to happen? She and her children were going to leave earth in a hot air balloon. For them, there was an apprehension, they were quiet, they had had time to think, but for her it was giddy excitement. Once the balloon, a dazzle of primary and secondary slices of colour had been unrolled and positioned and the whooshing gas started to fill it, they climbed into the wicker basket, not dissimilar to the PE basket at junior school where the skipping ropes and the bean bags were stored, but with partitions like a wine basket. Effortlessly, the inflated patchwork bladder began to rise from the ground, all the time, drifting away from the urban sprawl and the snaking motorway, leaving her husband and Nina to photograph the ascent and chase the balloon around the country lanes to its landing in Wilstead. In the basket everyone was taking photos and waving until those on the ground were nothing more than tiny specs.

It was simply amazing, the most perfect morning, the sun pushing through a bank of high stippled cloud, a gentle wind in which to drift silently across Bedfordshire. The unrestricted view was breath taking. There were no edges, no window frames, no kerbs, no borders, no boundaries, no painted lines, no gaps, no rules, nothing to interrupt or spoil. All round the balloon, the big empty sky stretched on for miles. Their voices trailed away to be consumed in the silent emptiness and apart from the occasional whoosh of gas to keep them air-borne it was unbelievably calm and eerily quiet.

As they climbed higher, they left behind them a scattering of farms and isolated houses, villages became miniaturized, traffic soundless, garden ponds blinked back in the sunlight, dots of sheep huddled, fields of oilseed rape, wheat and pasture were no longer identifiable, becoming nothing more than a patchwork of shaded greens, a black zip of track cut the land in half and a train slipped silently south.

Landing as they did in the crouched position in the basket compartments, the earth came all too soon into focus and back to reality. Brushing the canopy of a lone beech tree, its buds still waiting to burst they drifted and dropped to the ground. The basket dragged through the wet grass and lurched to a standstill in the dewy meadow, laced with spider's webs and lush with milkmaids and buttercups. Trembling and breathless, they crawled out of the basket. The excitement was washed down afterwards with a glass of champagne. A year later, she still thought about the balloon experience and her wonderful day.

There were days and days of much needed rain. A great swathe of isobars, tightly packed, circled the UK bringing at times torrential rain and driving winds. She used the time to explore the cavernous warehouses of B&Q, Homebase, Wicks, and Ikea – cathedrals dedicated to DIY. In Ikea she declined the bag handed to her at the top of the escalator. It was rumoured that no customer left without the need to purchase something. The need for a new oven had sent her to check out the current trends. Really, the flooring needed replacing too. In fact the whole kitchen needed an overhaul. So she found herself in the kitchen departments opening drawers and cupboards of the pretend fitted kitchens. Wet days were perfect for stripping wallpaper. It was her plan to restore her children's rooms to the floral chintzy look that they had been before they were born. So while attending to the needs of the kitchen she also looked at the wallpapers.

The day trip to Paris had been booked well in advance and she set the clock for 2.15am, time enough she thought for getting ready. For a few days her husband had been checking the forecast, there was nothing he liked more than having a reason to track the progress of the weather, it must be a compulsive disorder, and it wasn't promising. The weather map showed great swathes of rain and cloud hanging over northern France. It had been her intention to go in a summery, but not too summery dress and a little cardigan and not look like a regular English tourist. In the end she succumbed to the inevitable dependable jeans. Her husband had volunteered to take her and her friend to the station to catch the train at the ungodly time of twenty to four. When she whispered "It's five to three" and "It's time to get up," there was a great sigh from the cocoon of bed-covers and he probably wondered why he had.

She had first heard about the Channel Tunnel nearly forty years ago and thought at the time that it would be amazing to get on the train four miles away and travel to the rest of the world without getting off. She thought she remembered it being promoted that the train would travel from the Midlands and elsewhere in so many hours to the continent. In fact it didn't quite work out like that as a one stop tube journey or a short walk or a two stop bus journey intervened. On arrival, Euston station was silent, there were only a handful of people left over from the night before and everything was closed and shuttered, no-one checked their tickets. Outside it was raining and keeping any law and order on the hairstyles was quickly dismissed. They walked the short way to St Pancras International. It was the first time she had travelled on Eurostar. The train itself was nothing swishy unlike the startlingly fine station it departed from and once the formalities were completed the three friends boarded the train and settled into their seats.

Too busy gossiping they failed to notice the English countryside slip passed, then, suddenly the occupants of the carriage seemed to observe in unison. "We're in France." As predicted, festering cloud clung to the thin flat land either side of the train. The acres of wheat and oil seed rape was not a landscape that called for their attention and so they turned it towards their breakfast of salmon and cream cheese bagels served with champagne, opened discreetly in the leaning this way and that train. There were no particular plans for the day, although before they became too inebriated they hoped, like the previous week, to go to a gallery and soak up some culture. The queue waiting to go into the Musee d'Orsay was too long to wait in. They hadn't got all day and so went for a coffee, where the waiter slapped the cups and saucers roughly on the table because they had turned down his linked sale of croissants. Revising their route, they went instead to the Musee de l' Orangerie where the queue was much shorter, to feast on the Monet's and the Impressionists-her favourite style.

She had always admired the forthright simplicity of their 'ready-to-go' work, it had a freedom and was bravely honest, the artists not appearing to worry about the finer details or being too accurate. She liked the immediateness, the simple naivety of the paintings. Their work demonstrated the mood of the time, something radical and revolutionary. She liked to think that she could paint like them, bold colours and clumsy brush strokes; initially making a mess and saying it was done when she lost interest.

Monet's impressive canvases of life-size ponds hung on vast arcs of clear white space. She felt integral to the dappled water and the reeds and the lilies which, when she peered at them closely were nothing more than a whip of thick pink or creamy white paint whipped round with a one-inch brush.

After their cultural enlightenment it was time for lunch and they walked through Jardin des Tuileries towards Rue Montmorency, taking photos of the Tour Eiffel shrouded in low cloud, and the Arc de Triomphe suffused in the misty distance. It was easy to imagine the occupation, the wide grey boulevards packed with troops stretching along Des Champs Elysees, the fear and uncertainty. They lunched in the oldest house in Paris, Auberge Nicolas Flamel, built in 1407. The restaurant was laid with snowy damask cloths and napkins, the tables intimate, garnished with a rose or a cactus. For them the wine was expensive; so they chose a bottle of Bordeaux, the cheapest, the last one on the list, and the set menu. The food was artistically served with great detail paid to the presentation. The neat goat's cheese starter looked like a miniature spring garden, in perfect proportion, even down to the violet and spike of chive, now there was a use for those feisty little violets that plagued the borders at home, she could eat them and the shallot topped with the teasing raspberry standing aside the thick slice of duck that relaxed in a red onion chutney and the delicate pistachio tart. The whole proceeding was delightful and all too soon it was time to make their way back to the station. A steady rain had settled over Paris. They pondered over the wines in the duty free shop, choosing in the end the one with the screw top rather than the grape variety or the region it came from. The gossiping continued all the way back to London where they found it still to be drizzling and depressingly gloomy – not that they were. Old enough to know better, but drunk enough not to care they donned their cheap and cheery berets bought in Rue de Rivoli and instead of going to Euston, went laughing and giggling like three silly girls into the Skinner's Arms. One of her friends knew the area opposite Euston well, her grandmother and an aunt had lived there and she was keen to share her memories with her friends. Her grandmother's house across the road from the pub had a wide black front door with a black knocker, there were four floors and in those days there were a corresponding number of raps for each floor. Further on, at The Lord John Russell where they had another drink and patriotic bunting fluttered was her aunt's house and she recalled climbing over the spiky topped railings. It was dark and wet and time to go home. What a good day. The next trip was loosely arranged, it was just a case of deciding when.

It was the last day of April, the perfect day. After weeks of dismal weather, the sun came out from behind the cloud and it was warm. She cleared the chairs from the kitchen and washed the floor. It was worth explaining that as a rule she didn't wash the kitchen floor, admittedly it didn't show the dirt but remembered her mother being a slave to her one square metre of multi-coloured cushion flooring, a new product in its day. In the flooring department she had to stay cool and stand back from specs and marks, unlike her mother who, without fail vacuumed the carpets, shook the mats and scrubbed the scullery floor on her hands and knees every day before going to work at 7.45am. She hung the washing to billow and flap in the fresh air, she vacuumed the entire house. Upstairs, she inched the wardrobe to the centre of the room and pulled and pushed the great lumbering mattress that lolled this way and that to the room that she had tidied two weeks ago along with a stubborn chest of drawers. She turned the bed on its end. Even though she wasn't quite ready she took the step ladders from the garage and carried them upstairs ready to paint the ceiling. Once satisfied that all traces of wallpaper had been removed she vacuumed the carpet, preferring to leave the room as clean and tidy as possible. By lunch time she was out in the garden weeding and sweeping. No sooner were they beautiful when shattering rain and destructive squalls ravaged the crab apple and flowering cherry, snatching and snapping at their branches. The devastation lay everywhere. On the gravel beneath the trees, petals carpeted pink. She cut the grass with a push mower. It was hard work, slipping because it was still too wet and had grown too long because constant rain had prevented its regular cut. Filling the car with bags of weeds, she went to the dump.

2

It was the 1st of May and again it was raining. Returning to her decorating preparation she rubbed down the walls with sandpaper wrapped round a little wooden block. Over her face was a thin dusting of pale powder and her hair was sticky and matted with old plaster. To rid herself of the dust, she went for a swim.

It was probably more than ten years since she started to go to the pool on her own. It was when she and her son had the habit of watching 'East Enders' together, and, incidentally, coincided with Cindy frequenting her local pool to escape Ian and the children and indulge in an affair with the lifeguard, Matt. Having only gone to the pool with children in tow, or when she was a teenager, with friends, she was apprehensive, but bravely went on and off, overcoming her anxiety. Now it would seem odd to go with anyone and it surprised her that apart from families most adults did go alone. When on holiday abroad she swam on her own in the early morning before her husband was awake. A thousand thoughts and what ifs filled her mind, leaving her clothes on the end of a beach chair or on a rock, along with the all-important keys. What if someone stole them or they became lost in the sand? What if she was carried out to sea? What if she got cramp? What if she drowned? What if she disappeared? Of course none of those things would happen, locals were innocently walking their dogs or jogging or strolling in the cool of the morning before the sun took up its position for the day.

How quickly the water stilled, yet the slightest dip of a toe sent a gathering shiver across the pool. It was rarely glassy calm. Little slaps of white light danced and twinkled on the trembling surface. In the morning the distorted reflection of the windows shimmered along the length of the pool, pulsating up and down with the frequency of a busy oscilloscope reading. Swimmers and flapping children broke the water into choppy waves that spewed over the side into the drainage grating. Sometimes there was a strange smell, a stale pollution of unwashed kit left fermenting at the bottom of a bag, or a suffocating blend of incontinence and digestive biscuits. The acoustics beneath the surface were primaeval. Apart from her breath escaping and the deep dull primitive resonance there was no other sound. She loved the feel of the water, twirling around her like a roll of silk, holding her weightlessly or the rush of a million bubbles in the slipstream of another swimmer when they fizzed against her skin. It encompassed her yet it was undisturbed. Submerged below the unsteady light she could see the black tiles disappearing into the distance like a runway, legs and arms, people swimming under her, people waiting to catch a ball, mothers holding their babies. Surfacing the turbulence for air between strokes, broken snatches of the real world, voices, background music and splashing, replaced the echoing silence. Like being in a harder gear, she liked the resistance of pushing and pulling against the solid wall of water. For some, it was all about speed and racing against the clock, checking their water resistant watches. She was not an aggressive swimmer, no more than she was an aggressive driver, preferring her own steady regular rhythm, stopping or changing direction if need be, unlike some who created a tidal surge barging through regardless or pushed away from the side in a great biblical wave, impressive until they swam like a breathless tadpole. Slipping under water sometimes took courage, it could be too cool, but once submerged she soon adjusted. With one huge lungful of breath she exhaled a great jumble of bubbles, the amplified effervescence gushing and gurgling in her ears. It was the sound of being alive, yet not speaking. For her, swimming was calming. It really was an opportunity for people to shed their phones, their I-phones, to remove their ear plugs, to relax and get away from their frenetic lives for an hour. She understood that there were, like watches, music devices that were water resistant, but the most people she saw at the pool were like her, purely swimming for pleasure.

She didn't know that she had a technique, she just swam as well as she could, but as she grabbed the rail at the steps ready to launch herself from the water a swimmer waiting at the end of the lane to catch her breath said "I like your technique." And although she knew very little about strokes they proceeded to talk for a moment about them. Briefly she explained that a couple of years ago she had had lessons to learn primarily how to crawl. When later she said to her teacher that she found it exhausting, he suggested that she swam as slowly as possible. And so she developed the 'technique' that was suddenly of interest.

Being a senior citizen entitled her for the time being, to a reduction in the cost of public swimming sessions and she invested in a laminated super-saver card which reduced it still further. During term time there was a two hour slot for public swimming over lunchtime, when the pool was cordoned off into a fast lane and a slow lane for adults only and general swimming. She made good use of using the slow lane but in a funny way there seemed to be a pressure to swim non-stop, either too fast or too slow depending on the other swimmers and although she had to swim in between others, the main part of the pool was less restricting. Also, she felt that when it was busy, the lanes were very slightly too narrow and she was afraid of kicking someone or being kicked, as she was the other day by someone's overstretched leg. Occasionally when she missed someone by a whisker a pin-pricking tingling sensation radiated through her, as though a mini electric shock had passed between them and sometimes she grazed her little toe on the rope or hit her elbow on the wall. The school summer holiday brought with it a different routine.

The first week of the holidays brought with it a flush of hot weather. Opening times changed to accommodate more public swimming and the lunch-time slot was temporarily dissolved.

As it would be too busy she went at different times. Waking early on Friday morning, feeling the mattress piping beneath her curled knees and with barely more than a selvedge and a fringe of covers as her husband had hoisted them all on his side, she got up and went for an early swim. Not having a pre-paid card for the early session, she handed over her £4. The floors were dry and she headed for her usual cubicle along the back wall and locked the door. Used to the limited space, no more than a cupboard she perched her bag on the narrow shelf, no more than a plank for a thin child to sit on or dry your toes. Soon into her swimsuit and hat she carefully repacked her bag so that it would fit into the equally narrow locker. Because of the space restriction she used old football club towels belonging to her children. She had used them for years, not for their absorbency that's for sure, they had practically none-the pile was wafer thin, nor for their comfort as they felt as unforgiving as cardboard, but two of them rolled up fitted into her bag, also if they fell on the floor, it didn't matter whether she washed them, which was not often, or not, they quickly dried to a crisp. The almost indestructible black boxy bag, bought from a charity shop in the high street years ago was the perfect size and shape for the width of the bench and the width of the locker and fitted neatly in her bike basket if she used her bike and more importantly, it accommodated her mean towels and the clothes that she shed while she swam. What she always intended to do and was not beyond her capabilities was to over sew a little pocket to the inside lining for her one pound coin and laminated card. She had noticed that since her retirement that her usual thirty lengths were completed in a shorter time. Not at all tired or puffed she swam for a further ten lengths, then thought, might as well make it fifty. Wow, she had never swum a mile before.

Making the most of the local facility she went at least twice a week and although only a ten minute walk away she usually went in the car, mainly because the thought of meeting someone she knew when her hair was wet and straggly, her lipstick vanished along with her eyebrows and red eyes was worse than the getting out of bed in the morning look.

Going frequently she soon recognised faces and occasionally heard a name splashed about. People swam without limbs. Almost comical, the prosthesis, from the knee down stood amongst the energy drinks at the shallow end. Not one to talk at the end of lengths, preferring to plough on, up and down up and down, she rarely said anything more than hello, or smile. Over time she learnt their names and more about them. Marilyn who loved the adrenalin rush and the feel-good factor afterwards, the benefits far outweighed the effort and Gordon and Kate whose arthritis benefited from the exercise. Showering with Rick at the end of a lunchtime mile, she learnt that he was a stalwart of the model aeroplane enthusiasts. At the over 50s session she met Nicki, who with the best of intention had hoped to swim regularly but like her found that the discipline and commitment of trying to maintain any sort of continuity proved impossible at times.

She wore a hat to protect her hair and goggles to protect her eyes; not especially flattering. As the silicon hat relaxed on her great pile of hair it folded her ears and hoisted up, taking with it the loose lined skin, the ultimate, instant face lift. It gave her smooth elfin features, crease-free and uncharacteristically youthful. Her smiling mouth curved in a permanent state of happiness. On went the goggles, gripping her head, clenching her eyes, pressing in and denting the thin skin, leaving red wealds for at least an hour. Sometimes the water compressed against the goggles and she had to stop and lift them from her face to reduce the pressure. She had tried going without the goggles but didn't like the nip of the chlorine. Sometimes, for no apparent reason one side of her goggles would fill up like the little window on the kettle, gradually drowning her eye until she closed it. Reaching the end of the pool she would lift the flooded lens and tip out the water.

It was a straight forward pool, 33 metres x 15 metres, no flumes or slides. Blue tiles were divided into lanes with black, with a broken line nearing the ends to remind competitive swimmers or swim club swimmers or 'ordinary' swimmers the proximity of the wall. A set of steps marked the corners. Some children complained that it was boring, that they weren't allowed to do anything except swim, in other words jumping and diving in was not allowed. They were allowed a ball and other floating fun, and some played ingenious games underwater. Big windows opened onto a grassy area, seriously underused in 2012, more importantly for her was that she could see the sky and the clouds, blustering through or hanging like a shroud or high and wispy white. In the early morning, so often the best part of the day, the sky was a wall to wall canvas of blue, so full of promise.

She remembered it being an outdoor pool, taking her children and a picnic, spending the day or a few hours after school and coming home tired and weary. It was when wagon wheels were substantial.

She preferred not to say that swimming and walking were the mainstay of her exercise routine, but that somewhere they were included as part of her day. She did not want them to become an addictive or compulsive regime; if for a few days she didn't do either, it was no big-deal, but at the same time they had to be done often enough to avoid aching arms and legs. Both made her warm and stretched out her limbs. She varied her walks from day to day. It was her intention to walk Bury Common, a vast expanse of common land, 180 acres, convenient for dog walkers. She had walked it a few times, but not for a long time and certainly not on her own. She needed to feel confident walking alone because her husband's left knee was unpredictable and sometimes let him down, also his pace was much slower than hers and although quite happy to saunter with him, it was not what she called a walk. Any one of her long lean sons' stride was her only match.

Testing the feeling of walking alone, she hesitantly opened the clanging metal gate and took to the wide grassy path that was clearly visible fanning out and forking off in all directions. In all there were seven clanking gates, each reverberating when the catch was opened or closed, banging and vibrating, ringing round the field like a jungle drum when someone entered or left. As expected, people were walking their dogs. There was no turning back. It would have looked odd to suddenly change direction, as though she had forgotten something and turned hastily back. Years ago it would have seemed odd walking in the countryside alone unless you owned the land or were a poet or an artist or a vagabond or a shepherd. People just didn't walk about by themselves. They would stumble along verges and roads to get home or go somewhere but from being small she had had an irrational fear imprinted on her, that she might come to some terrible harm or be murdered or kidnapped if she was walking by herself.

Despite the bracing wind there were a few people about making the most of the bank holiday. She could see that dogs or the dog walkers could become her 'new' friends just as her husband had acquired 'new' friends. His friends all had the same name, Pete. In forty minutes her pace did not let up. Compared to the moors it was nothing, no more than a stamp of lumpy wasteland, a sprawl of rough undulating hillocks that rose away from the river, made-up of knotted grass and stubs of bush, outcrops of old hedgerows sprouting from ditches long dried up, herded trees and scattered copses. It was common land, thankfully protected against the onslaught of bricks and mortar that seemed to ravage and plunder onto any available piece of land. It had not always looked so common. Like other places, its rural idyll had been severely curtailed during the war in order to 'Dig for Victory' removing hedgerows and uprooting trees to provide land for agriculture and pasture for livestock to supplement the meagre rations. Locally, it was as close as she got to anything remotely wild. But even a few days later when bravely she was as far from civilisation as possible, there hanging in the air was the persistent cough of the motorway, and in the distance between the hedges, she could still see a fleeting glimpse of a car or a van and beyond that, the taller buildings and the church in the High Street. It was a glorious big sky afternoon. Chunky dandelions crouched, anchored firmly to the ground, and bright yellow celandines opened up their petals and turned their faces to the sun. Out of the wind, it was warm. Following the river to where the bank had been eroded and formed a wide shallow beach and a gentle slope into the water, where on a sunny day teenagers might wade in and cool off she turned left, back across a field and through another clanging gate then another field. Although weather-beaten and covered in velvety lichen, she could see that she might make use of the random seats dotted around in the summer months and take her book or her writing and romantically sit and while away the time. It was good that she had not been afraid. And if she had, she would have called her imaginary dog. "Here Bob, Bobby, here boy, where are you?" And he would come charging through the undergrowth by the fence, strands of glistening drool hanging from his jowls and growling in a frightening way.

Tuesday 1st May. By four when the sky lightened she put on her boots and went for a walk. Unexpectedly on Bury Common she met two friends and they stood, each holding their folded umbrellas, voicing opinions, airing their views and letting off steam about the sorry state of the economy, the spiralling cost of living, petrol prices, border control, local elections, water shortages, their children moving away only to return home again, 60 million people and there is no one to speak up for the people, 'ordinary people', those who regularly drink wine at £200 a bottle, simply have no idea how those people who drink wine costing £4.99 manage. Meanwhile, an excited dog came rushing around, rounding them up. The flooding curtailed her route and here and there the spongy ground was so waterlogged she had to backtrack. Three impatient ducklings left the safety of a branch dipping and bobbing in the surging river, drifting and swirling at a tremendous speed in the force of the current, their mother nowhere to be seen.

Friday 4th May. The kitchen had to last twenty years. After that, would it matter? She took a seat and leaned forward. Jamie who placed the order and was overseen by

Pete, who hardly intervened, had excellent customer care. She had her measurements ready and did not need the 'kitchen design service' that was available, claiming that she could measure, but non-the-less liked the back-up of the advisors. Her requirements were drawn out on a piece of A4 paper folded in half, dishwasher, front only 60cms, then 100cms for the sink, then 100cms for two cupboards then a 50cm cupboard/corner unit, the 60cms for the oven then 100cms for two cupboards then 30cms for a set of drawers and 40cms for a single cupboard in which she was going to store her extensive pile of magazines. That took her to the wall. Jamie placed the order and knew what she was talking about. She watched her scroll through the different components that she required, highlighting it then pasting it on her order. Once confirmed, it was neatly printed out and handed to her to sign. Pete leaned to his left and took out a presentation folder in which Jamie put the invoice. Having a 'new' kitchen was a step in the right direction. The reason for it being that the oven was continually producing a sooty deposit on the glass interior and her oven proof dishes and, although she never said, traces of soot glazed the food, too. It was time to call it a day. It was at least thirty years old. While in the store, she dealt with the flooring, 18sq metres of beige, wrongly described, more like stone coloured porcelain tiles. Using her retractable tape measure she had mapped out the area. She questioned Pete as the total appeared on the till. "From today it is 25% off all flooring this weekend." Wow. When the door slid open automatically under the Way Out sign, the sun was shining, lighting up the car-park. In due course it was delivered scanned and zapped and leaned underneath the stairs.

Sunday 6ᵗʰ May. Wearing her duffle and scarf and gloves, she took herself out for a brisk walk to clear the cobwebs that might settle if she didn't. Buttercups had pushed through to join with the new dandelions and the old ones that had gone to seed. Lady's lace had sprung up against the wire fence and behind, bluebells nestled under the trees. The network of grassy paths that merged and divided were even more obvious, beaten down where two sets of feet or one set and four paws had walked and squelchy in places from the recent rain. Shrinking back within its banks the river was once again contained but where it had spilled over, the long grass covering the banks was coated in a film of grey silt and leaned in the direction of the receding water. The turbid river was still brown and swollen, debris from somewhere else had become tangled and stranded in branches as the water swept through, in quieter spots it had eddied to form a floating cloth of dead reeds laid with a ball, a plastic bottle, broken chunks of polystyrene and a can. The pungent air hung with an earthy tang.

On Wednesday she painted the ceiling. Looking in the mirror at the end of the day when she cleaned her teeth and reapplied her lipstick before going to Aqua-Fit she could see that her face was stippled with white paint and where her hair had escaped the Vilene mob cap that, too, had been peppered. The next day, on her hands and knees, she rubbed and rubbed at the skirting, virtually removing the magnolia gloss painted years ago by her son when he wanted to exert his own ideas, to reveal the quiet willow green, mixed to match the floral Sanderson paper, hung nearly forty years ago.

A steady rain dimpled the already brimming pond. The ground was saturated, the army of water butts were filled to capacity, drowning. Like a drum, the rain beat steadily on the wooden sills and trickled along the gutter to dribble into the drain. Silver beads dripped from the wisteria branches that wove across the pergola. Initially dashes of rain struck the window but then it increased to roll down the glass in streaming ribbons. Tyres hissed in the accumulating surface water. Where they trailed, trouser hems darkened. Dogs were wet. Sounding like chips in a deep fat fryer the rain would crescendo, then decrease to a gentle whisper.

Wednesday 9th May. All day a veil of drizzle persisted. Starved of sun the ferocious weather continued. From where she sat at the computer she could see that the meadow opposite had flooded. Swans drifted between the goal posts where only the other day a group of youths had bravely played football with their shirts off. In general the weather was awful.

Friday 11ᵗʰ May. Lurking in the bottom of the fridge, she could see that she had all the vegetables to make a hearty pot of minestrone soup; so she set to, peeling, slicing and dicing. When it was ready, she took herself out for a walk, making the most of the dry day. Leaving the house, she turned right and made her way round Riverside Meadow to Castle Meadow, across the river Ouzel and into the graveyard, having to walk amongst the leaning gravestones to avoid the flooding where the confluence of the Ouse and the Ouzel met, then through Ousebank Gardens to Mill Street, which unlike weekends was virtually empty of cars, the need to work to pay the mortgage clearly evident. The gate squealed on its hinges. Once again the river, in places, had escaped its banks, subdued over the already sodden ground but still brown and churning in full spate, swirling and surging where it was deeper, eating away at the edges. The detritus had been swept away. It was an exhilarating morning, bright, with a cool fresh breeze and clouds that rolled through without stopping. Walking against the wind she took great lungs of air, behind her, her hair stretched straight out like a flag. Out of the wind it was still, she was warm and unzipped her jacket. In the hedgerows, between the dancing heads of lady's lace, blue spikes of bugle competed for attention. And in the corner an outbreak of spiny backbones, last year's teasels leaned in the wind. Above her, there were skylarks. A fence and water filled ditch prevented her from going further. In a matter of weeks she had exhausted the various routes that traversed the field and although she would still walk there, she needed to expand her horizons and go further afield.

Clearing the shed, one of three, was long overdue. It was called the bike shed and undoubtedly it did contain bikes, though only one complete bike and that was hers, kitted out recently with a basket arrangement to accommodate local shopping. She wheeled it out and leaned it against the wall. The next bike was without handlebars, the brakes dangled freely. That, too, she leaned next to hers. From the hook she lifted her deck chair frame, in case it fell and folded her up in its grasp, leaning it, too, along with the bikes.

A huge box of wood off-cuts was blocking the way, piled high with the things that had fallen off the warped and sagging shelf that had partly collapsed but which still hung by a splinter to the sides of the long, narrow shed. Pieces of fine art lay rusted and strewn, rolled, folded and squashed – spoiling. Three garden chairs had been, for want of a better word, launched on top of the pile. There seemed to be umpteen pairs of wellingtons and perished waders and work boots coated in cement. She removed everything into the brightness of the day. The shelf came away easily. On the shelf above were great wedges of sound proofing foam and a biodegradable bag of trimmings which promptly fell apart on moving. Onto the empty shelf she tidied the art exhibits.

Behind the box there was a sun lounger along with its disintegrated cushion. Hoisting and pulling at it over the box was awkward, foam chips were falling all over the place, underneath it was a roll of left over carpet and on each side were numerous bike frames. With all her strength she heaved and pushed the box of wood to the end and on each side she lined-up the bike frames on their ends, all the spare wheels and tyres slotted between.

Everywhere there were signs of mice, nests, droppings and mice in various states of decay. Rigor mortis had stricken and their little slightly foetal-position bodies were rigid and tails set in a wiggly line where they finally dropped dead. Oozing liquid had stuck their fur fast to the carpet and quite rough treatment with the broom failed to budge them. For years it had been their playground, gnawing and nibbling, running around, playing dare with the 'Little Nipper' in the corner, getting caught, limping about, dragging the tortuous wooden trap along till desperation turned into death. It was unfortunate.

When she had swept and vacuumed, she rehung the deck chair frame on the peg, lifted the bike with no bars to lean on one side of the shed and her own she wheeled to lean on the other.

Filling her car she exiled the rubbish to the dump, the sun lounger went in the metal bit, the chip-board shelf went in the wood bit and everything else went into household waste, she did not hang about to be questioned about the contents of the sacks and bags. Finally peeling off her rubber gloves, she had a shower and put all her clothes in the wash.

Firstly, when she had finished gardening she would store the mower and tools in the shed at the end of the garden, peel off her rubber gloves and return them with her kneeling mat and hand fork to the porch, slip off her gardening trainers, as though she had a selection to choose from, whereas, alas, she only had one pair, left, courtesy of Becky. They had, however, stood her in good stead and looking at the state of them they were not going to last much longer. As it was the soles had lost their tread offering no grip on damp grass, and it wouldn't be the first time that she'd nearly slipped over, then she would wash her hands in the kitchen sink, run upstairs and then look out to admire the freshly turned soil, clipped grass, and manicured edges.

It seemed no time since the three conifers had been planted and although they had been kept trimmed and neat they had grown too big and outstayed their welcome. Darkening and filling the space they closed out the sky, and whilst there was room to do so, they needed to be lopped severely. Felling the conifers was a recipe for disaster. Her husband leaned the double extension ladder against the branches, climbed up and tied a rope around the bottom of the top ten feet. Picking up the saw he climbed up again. She stood on the bottom rung to give the ladder some stability. Nothing felt firm. Leaning in, with the saw in one hand he sawed into the bark. When nearly through she stepped off the ladder and taking hold of the rope, pulled with all her might to bring it to the ground. It was so dangerous; the weight of the great spinning-top of branches almost out of control could have toppled her husband.

Thankfully the lumberjacks lived to tell the tale and the pigeons lost their perches.

Sunday 13th May. The car insurance was due. The difference between the original quote and the new one was the lovely orange dress that kept appearing in her mind. The beautiful blue sky morning changed her mind about going to the shops and instead, she pulled on her boots and went out. She turned her walk around. Being Sunday morning there were lots of people about, walking their dogs, jogging, even a woman, like her, walking alone. Everything had grown. The grass was longer and folded in the wind, lady's lace had almost obscured a bench where disturbed dandelion clocks dispersed gently in the air. Around all the gates the puddles had dried to a potter's clay consistency, huddled boot prints, clearly imprinted, faced all directions. Walking the opposite way she saw a different view. In the distance, between the trees were triangles of gaudy rape seed and a herd of Friesians, intent on munching the lush new grass, rooks called and circled above their nests high in the ash trees. The path seemed as straight as a dog's hind leg and as she walked she faced into the breeze. That too had turned. The river had receded and instead of the rolling boil it was simmering, contained again within its banks. Like Lurex it spangled in the sunlight. Silver crests danced on the surface. On the far bank the swaying willows murmured as they dipped their fronds in the current.

Wednesday 16th May. Approaching the field, there were cars parked by the copse further on. From a distance she could see the area being staked out with red and white poles. Intrigued, it all became clear later when the paper dropped through the letterbox. It explained that an archaeological dig was needed to accurately determine the discovery, three years ago, of Iron Age/Roman remains found when digging the foundations for a new park bench. Instead of continuing around the field, she lifted the clattering latch and out of the kissing gate at the far end and into the narrow lane. After 200 yards it gave way to nothing more than a bridle-way leading upwards, a green corridor, splashing through the big slopping puddles was unavoidable. Sheltered and out of the wind it had its own micro climate. The undergrowth grew vigorously, uncontrolled, competing for space, fighting for survival. Here the lady's lace was as tall as her, branches reached and caught her hair, aggressive dark green nettles that surely could be a healthy substitute for spinach were twice the height, and weaving through and sticking to everything was goose grass. The track opened into a field and led eventually to a bridge over the river. She went no further. Back on the common, Ruby the boxer bounded heavily up behind her, her hands were at the same height as her open jaw and yellowing teeth. Ignoring the dog she paid it no attention but she didn't like it. The dog would know that. Then further on, there was a man and a dog, a smooth coated Weimaraner, on a photo-shoot against the backdrop of buttercups. The pampered dog sat and lay in several poses while its owner clicked away. Now where had she seen that? She thought. It was in Denver when she and her husband were waiting for the Museum of Natural Sciences to open. Now why should she be cynical? She was just as bad, taking photos of food. Walking around, she had hoped to use her new toy, a digital voice recorder. It was her intention to use it when she was out and about, to record her thoughts and ideas so that she didn't have to remember them or, as she had tried, write them down as she walked, or stopped completely to make a note. It was neat and slim like a mobile phone, but having resisted owning one, she had not overcome the feeling of talking into one. It was in her pocket along with a tissue and her keys. Feeling conspicuous, she could see people in the distance, at least half a mile away and she felt silly, so she didn't use it.

In order to improve her confidence, it had been recommended that should make use of one at a public speaking course that she had enrolled on, not so much to record her thoughts, but to hopefully improve her confidence when speaking in front of people. The mismatched furniture had been pushed aside. An arc of tables faced the whiteboard, where the day's three objectives had been scrawled. The windows were thrown open to enable a flow of air. She would have preferred to see rain shearing down against the glass as it was hard to concentrate on such a glorious spring day before the dull and dreary weather set in. The five students, eight had enrolled for the course, but maybe three had looked at the promising day and thought that they would give it a miss, were bombarded with an avalanche of information, and the analogy of standing under a waterfall and trying to have a drink was given. In comparison to the deluge very little would actually be swallowed. Pieces of paper were handed out and dutifully completed, fire exits and assembly points, toilets and vending machines were pointed out. Speaking in public set her pulse racing and frightened the life out of her and although she had done it many times she wanted to improve and continue, already she had a booking for January, but wanted to speak by then without the fear and dread that so beset her.

The Aqua Fit session on a Wednesday evening offered an energetic workout to music, designed to get the heart racing and the muscles toned. For half an hour they warmed-up and every now and then, Mandy, the teacher, said when she thought the class was flagging, you have got fifty minutes to go, or thirty six minutes left. She stood at the front of the class a few feet from the side of the pool. For the most benefit, it was advised to stand where the water came between the navel and the nipple line, so she lined herself up with the window frame. To avoid the bother of washing her hair at the end, she wore her hat. There was no feeling much worse than long wet straggly hair on a cold night. With all the jumping about that was involved she preferred to wear a swim suit, keeping all flesh firmly under control. Like many other ladies she bought her instantly recognisable and reasonably priced swimsuits in M&S, and maybe it would be better to buy a more expensive swim brand, but with constant use the colour quickly drained and the fabric lost its elasticity. Was it worth it? For ordinary swimming she also wore bikinis and although initially bought for holidays abroad, it seemed a pity to not to make use of them. It was inevitable but over time she went to Aqua Fit class less and less. While she was working, the class offered a midweek workout but more importantly, a distraction, but gradually, as 'ordinary' swimming increased, so the need lessened.

Friday 18th May. It was a lovely morning. As she crossed into Castle meadow, into her head came the fleeting memory of taking her cantankerous mother out in the wheelchair. She wasn't slight and manoeuvring her around was such hard work. But she took great pleasure from seeing the horse chestnut trees in all their glory as they were on that lovely morning. The voice recorder was in her shoulder bag and as soon as there was no one in sight she bravely spoke into it. Admittedly she still felt a little foolish, but from the practical point of view it was easier and she would become more comfortable using it. She spoke into it several times. A small copper butterfly basked in the warmth. Smudges of red clover were appearing, sedges and grasses were nudging taller and in the distance, trees were frothy clouds of green. Knowing all their names, she remembered collecting wild flowers when she was a child and entering the wild flower category in the annual horticultural show, held in the village hall. Along the hawthorn hedges, clusters of creamy May blossom were bursting, choking the air with its heady smell.

She loved seeing the room taking shape, the wallpaper spreading round the walls, the clear lines, meeting the ceiling – the sharp white edge – meeting the skirting board – the hard gloss line and the chaos of the upturned bed standing fatally wounded along with the wardrobe, displaced and huddled to the middle of the room. She noticed the join, the thin line lost in the pattern where each length butted against the next. She looked for it amongst the eau-de-nil sprigs. Even though they were fully aware when they bought the paper that the pattern repeat was 46cms they despaired and sighed at the waste each length that they hung generated. There were only so many drawers she could line. Just a glimpse of the finished empty room pleased her. It was never the same again, filled with the creases of an unmade bed, the trailing flex of the hairdryer and the general clutter of discarded clothes, the jumble of shoes along the skirting board, the hooks on the bedroom door draped with dressing gowns, pictures and drawers not quite closed.

Sunday 20th May. Another sunless day, a thick blanket of cloud spoilt the view that she knew so well. Instead, her eyes took in the foreground, passed pasture, lush with all the rain, a flock of sheep ambling, cattle munching, acid yellow fields of rape seed ready for harvesting and the trees, a fusion of greens, foaming into a hazy blur, their new growth reaching and stretching, claiming space, transforming and softening the silhouette and nearer to London, breaking up the harshness of warehousing, builder's yards and the old Victorian terraces, their gardens once lovingly tended, but now left to rack and ruin that fringed the track. Like seaside beach huts, abandoned carriages along the sidings were sprayed in glorious Technicolor graffiti. Approaching Inner London, towering buildings began to close in round her.

As always, in the end, the need for comfortable feet decided the dress code. In the morning, having hung her clothes ready the night before, she completely changed her mind. Assuring herself that she would get warm, she went meanly dressed. It was spring for God's sake.

Looking back, to what must seem to some to be like the Victorian era it would have been a disgrace to go to church in anything other than your Sunday best, hat and gloves, fully coordinated. Children, too, were dressed up and men were expected to wear a suit or a jacket and tie.

Beneath the table that separated them, the woman opposite was wearing black court shoes and smartly creased black trousers. Her royal blue mascara brushed onto her dark oriental lashes matched the blue in her scarf. Her hair was immaculate, anchored down with tiny clips and although she didn't need to, she whipped out a little folding mirror and reapplied her lipstick. And there she was sitting in her oldest jeans, cast-offs from a local charity shop, verging on threadbare. Then, rubbing salt into the wound, she took from her bag a very tattered tooled bible, open and closed so often that the well-worn fluttering pages were about to fall away from the spine. It was navy blue with faded silver writing on the cover, a narrow satin ribbon marked the page. None of her bibles, and she had several, had had such use. On reaching Euston, she was sad to leave the toasty warmth breathing from the grill at her feet.

Weaving from the station to Trafalgar Square the streets were empty, apart that is, from the tourists making an early start, lumbering suitcases growling behind them, and the street cleaners collecting rubbish and sweeping pavements of the excesses left by the public the night before. Nearing St Martins she could hear the bells pealing. She loved that sound. On reaching Pret a Manger, conveniently close to church, she was warm. Too warm to sit inside, so she took her breakfast of porridge and coffee to the scattering of tables overlooking the square.

Once seated, and with a few minutes to spare, she looked around. There were busy, purposeful little errands going on, offerings brought out from the vestry on a tray, candles being lit, toing and froing along the nave. Worshipers sat in ones and twos along the aisle. Not until just about 10 o'clock did the congregation swell. Observing them, there was no need to doubt the suitability of her clothes. There was a blue and white striped rugby top, a number nine emblazoned on the back, a leather jacket, hoodies, leggings, headphones, zipped tops with logos, crumpled sweatshirts pulled from the wash basket, digging-the-allotment jumpers, walking-the-dog jackets unhooked from the nail on the back door, great outdoor jackets and jeans. Let there be jeans. Alleluia.

At 11.30am, she met her son at the bronze rocking horse. Making use of her two for one bargain that she found while reading the leaflet picked up at the station, they decided on a visit to the Courtauld Gallery in Somerset House. Approaching from the Embankment side, the buildings flanked an almost empty piazza. Leaving the teeming commotion the almost empty courtyard was quiet and peaceful. Voices and the clink of coffee cups echoed from the clutch of cafes secluded in the shadows.

Again using the 2 for 1 offer they lunched at Navajo Joe in Covent Garden, eating spicy fajitas and chimi-changas washed down with a lager. Like an appendage, her umbrella adorned her wrist. She knew when she left home that it would be a nuisance.

She brushed and brushed at the little mark between her front teeth. It seemed that it had always been there, but in recent weeks she had spent too much time in front of the mirror and suddenly it seemed more noticeable. At her check-up she asked the dentist if it could be removed. The dentist explained that it was childhood decay and that it had stopped abruptly because of the fluoride in toothpaste and the natural bacteria in saliva. As though her teeth were rock formations she said that there was a good example on a back molar, adjusting the light she picked up a magnifying glass to show her.

Too quickly the holiday loomed and its preparation was well underway. Gathering on the dining room table were the essentials, passports, travel documents, camera, purse for the rupees, mosquito plugs, tea bags, travel wipes and insect repellents. Nothing was overlooked.

Upstairs, the shirts and shorts and summer dresses were airing. In another room, laid across the carpet were dresses and skirts half unpicked that she hoped if there was time, to restore. She and her husband went shopping. She tried on the orange dress that had been worth persevering to lower the insurance quote for. It was nice enough but for what it was, it was grossly overpriced. Instead she bought a spotted linen dress. Her husband went all eastern and bought two crumpled linen shirts; one a white collarless shirt, and one a buttery yellow. She went to the library and picked up a travel guide for India. She went to Boots and bought rehydration capsules. The cases were placed side by side on the end of the bed and filled with the accumulated clothes. After wishing her a good holiday Linda from the bank's parting shot was not to go near the rabid dogs. She replied that not even in England did she volunteer to go near any dog. Not a moment too soon she went for the all-important eyebrow tint and leg wax, as, since Monday, the sky had been cloudless. Although longing to whip the razor over her legs she refrained, wearing tights instead with her new summer dress when she met up with friends. As though it was a matter of life or death there was always a big effort to tidy and garden before holidaying, meals made the week before going away made use of random odds and ends so that the fridge was less empty than usual. While away, her children would call from time to time, so she made a batch of muffins that they could graze on as they passed through the kitchen for a couple of days – they would last no longer. Anxiety would set in and even though she had spoken to them, she left the customary note on the kitchen table: 'cut the grass, put water in the bird bath, water the plants, make sure everything is off and up and out and locked, signing off, love from mum x.' Her husband's apprehension about the problems earlier on the motorway was unfounded and in the end it was an effortless journey. They weighed their bags and checked themselves in, which, when it was first introduced a few years ago, added an additional stress to an already nervous tension. Until their flight at ten, they read and ate and people- watched. Gradually their flight moved up the departure board and they were called to the gate. To improve her chances of a more comfortable night ahead, she bought a neck pillow and although hot, it was slightly better. The seating was unbearably cramped, the armrests mean and hard. What do you do with your arms, cross them, fold them, stretch them out, hands splayed on thighs? Could there not be a bunk-bed arrangement on a long flight? Eventually the night ended with a mini breakfast presented on a tray. Nearly there.

Idly turning the pages of a weekend newspaper at the kitchen table back in February, they had been drawn to the Golden Triangle tour of India, visiting the Imperial cities of Delhi, Agra and Jaipur then to journey to the foothills of the

Himalayas a cultural cocktail suffused in hazy pink. The photographs were mesmerising, the itinerary mystical and exciting, like stepping into another world and so by Thursday the following week it was booked at the local travel agents. It prompted images of shaded pavilions and minarets and memories of Commonwealth Day at junior school when pupils were expected to dress-up in costumes from Commonwealth countries. And even though by then India was no longer under British rule, it was still represented.

Along with another couple from Kent, Surendra met them at Delhi airport. They stood in the shade in a draught of hot wind. Within moments, while waiting for Amrik to pull-up with the mini-bus they wilted in the oppressive heat. All the way to the hotel, Surendra talked about the government buildings that lined the wide roads, their architecture and history. For the entire week he was a mine of information, there was nothing he didn't know about. He waxed lyrical about dates and names and places and artefacts, proud to show them his country. He knew about farming, law and order, health, the government, sport, current affairs, industry, religion and the caste system and the differences between each region.

Nothing that she had read in glossy guides or seen on TV prepared her for her first glimpses of the destitution and deprivation that spilled into view along the Mehrauli Badapur Road. People lived in the most squalid conditions along the edges of roads in make-shift tents of plastic sheeting, sacks and bits of cloth flung over branches. They sat in the dirt, in the torrid heat, waiting. Everywhere was strewn with rubbish and rubble. Over everything there was a layer of dust, blown about by the relentless mad chaotic traffic. Open sewers and drains only a breath away. Stagnant ditches and toxic ponds were clogged with floating debris some of which were noxious green, some poisonous black. Cattle, pigs, goats, camels, donkeys and mangy feral dogs roamed freely, defecating and urinating, rooting amongst the waste. Like the people, they seemed to have no fixed purpose. Further on some hopefully set out stalls on the side of the road in the beating sun, selling water melons or lychees that they doused regularly with tainted discoloured water drawn from the fly infested tap in the market. To her it was appalling.

Whole communities lived in urban shanty towns, on what we know as land-fill sites, spending their time sifting through the garbage, pocketing rat-infested remains of those who were more affluent. People had absolutely nothing. They had no sanitation and no running water. They sat on their haunches or simply gave up and lay down in the filth. What clothes they wore were stained grey and stiff with dirt. On the platform in Delhi station amongst the commotion and frantic clamouring, people lay down anywhere, maybe hoping never to wake and face yet another day. Would anyone care? Would anyone notice? As their train pulled away she noticed a woman lying crumpled on her side, malnourished, no flesh on her bones, her feet bare, ingrained with dirt, her hair like tufts of raw wool, a little heap of rags. It was pitiful. It was heart-rending. The foetid smell was one of hopelessness, a tired, worn out smell of degradation, a heady acrid concoction of humans, animals, sewerage and the baking airless heat. Being privileged to air conditioned hotels and mini-bus meant that she rarely breathed the hot stale air. At Delhi station despite holding her breath for as long as possible, it was enough to make her want to wretch. Her senses were heightened in the noise and the squalor and the filth. Hand in hand with the grinding poverty was the desperate plight of the beggars, the hawkers and the street children who emerged from the hooded shadows of the shabby chaos as soon as a potential customer appeared, well versed and persistent, pestering to sell necklaces and glittering elephants and tacky plastic toys. They were difficult to avoid and even more difficult to refuse.

The trip was called the Raj Tour which naturally meant that a good deal of travelling was involved. It was a restless land. Like a massive exodus everything was on the move, bumper to bumper, if they had a bumper, roads were clogged with traffic, impatient and competing for space, inching forward, finding a gap, taking a chance, risking a life. There were five lanes of traffic in a two lane road agitating and vying for position, all the time a commotion of horns honking and peeping. Few vehicles were free from scrapes and dents, wing mirrors were wrenched off or taped down, bumpers loose and dangling. Whole families rode on scooters, father steering, the two children, sitting astride their arms fastened round each other, then mother sitting behind, side saddle in her flip-flops and bag over her shoulder, a flash of colourful sari streaming behind. In Delhi green and yellow tuk-tuks (auto-rickshaws) cluttered the roads. Compelled to take a ride in one, she and her husband braved the fug, the claustrophobic congestion, the noise and the mayhem. It was not for the feint-hearted. The pollution was so bad that bikers and cyclists wrapped and tied bits of cloth over their mouths and noses or apart from their eyes, mummified their entire head with bandaged tablecloths. Leaving Jaipur, elephants on their way to Amber Fort, walked amongst the thronging traffic, some carried sugar cane in their trunks. Between Jaipur and Delhi major road works caused delays, the journey taking longer than expected. For the site staff it was sandals and saris. Safety was largely ignored, no hard hats, no high 'viz' jackets, no cones or barriers. Driving was a free for all, a race against time, jostling for position, a slalom of manoeuvers, overtaking, undertaking, round the chicane, slipping on the gravel, when there was a broken down truck jacked up or an oncoming truck on the wrong side of the road, drivers would drive along the verge to get round it causing a great swirling cloud of yellow dust or when impatience proved too much in the shade-less heat, they simply turned off the highway and drove across the fields. To arrive unscathed was a bonus. There were no rules or if there were they were blatantly disobeyed. From camel carts laden with wood to container lorries and canvas-covered trucks, their cabs gaily painted and decorated with pom-poms and tinsel, Chaudhary Transport, Neemrana, Neer AJ Patel and of course China Shipping, bony brown elbows resting on the mean open window or space where there might have been one. Along stretches of road were garage workshops for the much needed repairs boasting great piles of threadbare tyres and to escape the scorching 45° heat and the bleaching white light men rested in the shade under their lorries leaving their engines to cool. Broken down lorries and burnt out trucks were frequently abandoned at the side of the road and left to rust. In an effort to keep to their schedule, the overcrowded buses squeezed through the chaos, brown curtains were sucked from the open windows flapping and writhing in the baking hot wind. On the way to the Jahangir Palace bus loads and bus loads of people were returning from a pilgrimage, they didn't worry about comfort and maximum 8 standing passengers, they all piled in, and when it was stuffed to capacity, they sat on top or once they had a foothold they just hung on. In places at the side of the road, swarms of fizzing flies feasted on the carcasses of the sacred cattle that had inadvertently strayed onto the road to be struck by a passing lorry. Leaving Delhi for Shimla they took the Shatabdi Express to Chandigarh to continue by road through the foothills of the Himalayas. The train was efficient and on time. Taped to each carriage was a faxed print-out of names, mainly Indian passengers and amongst them, was theirs. Within moments of departing, two wiry little Indians brought a litre of water to each person followed by a tray of snacks and a Thermos of tea, then no sooner had the tray been collected than the three course meal, was prepared in the 'pantry' car and served hot, in foil containers. Although the staff urged them and perhaps felt disappointed that they did not participate, they didn't eat, the lure of the toilet afterwards being too off-putting.

Between the commotion in the towns and cities, it was reassuring to see rural areas more productive. Towards Mathura no land was left to waste, parched fields were neatly farmed and waiting for the monsoon. In order to be able to cook on an open fire women made patties out of dung and stored them in what looked like round mud houses. They looked like a giant size version of what Sarog called a 'spicy fairy cake'. They carried them in round shallow containers on their heads. Great bundles of reed and firewood were also carried in this way. In the mountains every available piece of land was terraced and farmed.

To be honest, apart from the call centres that annoyingly rang when she was just about to serve dinner and a handy jar of Patak's Jalfreizi paste and the coal burning pollution that was belting out destroying the ozone, India did not particularly feature in her day. But listening to Surendra and Denesh awakened her senses and stirred her memories, childhood memories. India came to life again. Deep in the back of her mind India had been a world of fiction, of myth and legends, of poetry and stories, of princesses and jewelled slippers and domed palaces and sultans riding on elephants. Old enough to remember celebrating Commonwealth day at school, she like the other children, dressed up in costumes depicting those worn by indigenous peoples, grass skirts, cork brimmed hats, turbans and blackened faces. It was in the days of Rhodesia, before Zimbabwe. The Silk Road bubbled to the surface, as did the Khyber Pass and the Mughals and the Ottoman Empire and the Himalayas. Tea and cotton and rubber and the East India Docks on the Thames came into her mind. Returning home from the hazy hubbub, she was full of India. Bursting with tastes and sights and sounds, she reached for an encyclopaedia on the bookshelf, alas so old that it was not in colour, but depicted in grey, India was part of the British Empire. Then by chance when flicking through the channels because his favoured team the Republic of Ireland were failing miserably in their first match, her husband found 'The Idiot Abroad'. The idiot just happened to be in India. And so she put aside what she was doing and perched on the edge of her seat and watched.

The itinerary more than lived-up to the mirage so long forgotten. She knew that she sounded presumptuous but it was hard to describe the forts and palaces without writing like a travel guide, or a historian, or a museum curator, tending to choose the same describing words. She could be forgiven, seeing that she too was bowled-over, it was to be expected. Words alone didn't do the cultural sites justice. The picture needed noise, dazzling bright light, deepening shadows and the unforgiving heat to give it its edgy atmosphere.

Leaving the hotel at five, they captured the Taj Mahal in its early morning glory. It was breathtakingly exquisite. In perfect symmetry it stood serene and cool as it had for over three hundred years. Against the bluest of skies kites spiralled on thermals around the confection of slender minarets and perfect cupola. Clad in gleaming white marble quarried in Makrana, the Moghal Mausoleum was utterly intoxicating. Bathed in low sun the intricate opalescence of the inlaid mother of pearl shimmered. Its peacefulness reflected in the formal pond in the foreground. Inside, fretted marble screens protected the tombs that were decoratively inlaid like fine embroidery in precious stone, agate, lapis lazuli, carnelian, onyx and green chrysolite.

Jahangir Palace was moated to keep out the raping and pillaging invaders. As an added deterrent crocodiles once lurked below the surface. Built in sandstone the vast courtyard was surrounded by richly carved pillars and shady arches, exquisite arabesques adorned the marble walls. Fatehpur Sikri, also built of sandstone was elaborately carved and on the great sandstone slabs of the courtyard was a huge chequered board where the slave girls were used as parts of the game. In Jaipur the Maharaja's Palace was made up of interlocking rooms and courtyards that at the time were spread with carpets and hung with drapes and are used now to house the museum. Weapons, carpets, costumes, paintings and state regalia make most of the collection. It was Surendra who brought the buildings to life, describing in careful detail the lavish lifestyle and domestic arrangements within the walls, beautiful knotted wool carpets, silk curtains, silk carpets in the summer months, dripping chandeliers, cool air devices worked by the cool air wallah, plumbing arrangements worked by the water wallah, baths, and swimming pools, kitchen arrangements to suit vegetarians and meat eaters, the gardens, growing and supplying the needs of the establishment.

Just the name Palace of the Winds (Hawa Mahal) in Jaipur was evocative, a beautiful hollow façade of niches and windows in pink sandstone, where the royal women could overlook the swarming bazaar below without being seen. They did go to the Observatory and check the time but the savage heat too quickly sapped their energy and the ride in the rickshaw was totally abandoned. It was the day that India was shut, protesting against the high price of petrol. They visited the step well at Abhaneri, an amazing feat of precision engineering, showing the finest craftsmanship.

Along with the Taj Mahal, the mighty hilltop Amber Fort had to be a highlight, remembered especially because of the decorated elephants garnished in red throws that plodded their way carrying visitors up the steep cobbled path to the Fort. On entering through the massive gate a flourish of drums added drama to the throbbing excitement and welcomed the visitors. Again the stonework was complicated and the marble inlaid. Within the Fort, the pillared pavilions were lavished in mirror and stained glass. Faded pictures painted on wet plaster, adorned the walls.

Before visiting the Friday Mosque in Old Delhi they removed their sandals and slipped on a pair of disposable slippers. Women, not suitably covered were dressed in the shady entrance by the wardrobe wallah in hideous garish shrouds. Preferring to walk barefoot, she declined the slippers. In the respectful quiet she was aware of the slap of feet on the smooth warm stone. Within moments, the dry gritty air was exhausting. Overlooking the meat market, kites wheeled in anticipation. Along the road towards Mahatma Gandhi's memorial at Raj Ghat they saw their first working elephant swinging along in the merciless traffic. Before leaving for Agra their last stop was the WW1 War Memorial Arch built to commemorate those who died as part of the British Empire. Driving from Agra on the border of The Northern Plains into the arid region of Rajasthan, just that bit nearer to Pakistan and Afghanistan and Iran, the 'unsettled' hotspots in the world was a little bit daunting, concluding that place names and countries sounding 'an' at the end were all tarred with the same brush and to be avoided. Looking out over the dusky city later in the week from the bar on the roof, open to the hot, stifling evening air, it was easy to picture the unrest not a world away, the crumbling buildings, barbed wire, people scurrying or sitting in the shadows, burnt out cars, sporadic gunfire, a dog barking. Another gin and tonic was ordered. Travelling north to Shimla was different again. All the way to Chandigarh her husband was anxious, convinced that they would be stranded and bewildered on the heaving platform and left to fend for themselves. As they pulled into the station and the train shuddered to a stop there was Rowinder, exactly as arranged, holding up their names in bold black type. Her husband's relief melted the tension and without delay Rowinder soon had them out of the frantic station and into the waiting taxi.

Nestled against the sides of the mountains, high amongst the foothills of the Himalayas, Shimla was a refuge from the searing heat of the south. It felt like the top of the world. The town smacked of British Colonialism. After the 'toy train' experience, Dinesh showed off the Viceregal Lodge, now the Indian Institute of Advanced Study, draped in wisteria and built in true Scottish style. They walked round the very peaceful rose garden. They breathed deeply. Inside, the guide who spoke in English and Hindi drew their attention to the lofty walnut ceiling and the carved teak panelling and the conference room, hung with wallpaper from Maples in Tottenham Court Road, where Ghandi, Nero and Lord Mountbatten concluded the British rule. Surprisingly Dinesh spoke proudly of those times.

'I keep six honest serving-men

(They taught me all I knew)

Their names are What and Why and When

And How and Where and Who.' "Just so stories" Rudyard Kipling

Dreams disturbed. She lay awake, listening to the night, to the unfamiliar sounds, yet feeling safe on the earth, the steady thrum of the air-conditioning, wake-up calls, the plumbing, car horns, sirens howling dogs, whispering trees, birds roosting, power clicking off and on again, the haunting moody call to prayer. She thought of the teeming slums and the people living in their makeshift tents and the contrast of her in a hotel wanting for nothing, somehow it felt uncomfortable. Observing the caste system didn't seem right either. All human beings deserved to be treated equally, they were all the same. She was not better than them but was spoilt with attention, wanting for nothing, flushed with a lavish lifestyle, choice, water, air-conditioning and food. She used the time to think about the day. She thought about those Indian names that she couldn't pronounce and she would look up from the register and recognize the face and smile and place a tick beside the name she couldn't say. She remembered Shamila, Shimla's original name, who used to give her acupuncture and she had seen houses and boats with names like Kerela.

Meeting after a drink at the Oberon, Rudyard Kipling's haunt, not forgetting Michael Palin's too, Dinesh took them on a heritage walk, taking in the colonial buildings, The Mall and the Church. Standing high overlooking the town was the Hanuman Temple. It was nice not to be hassled and bothered by hawkers and beggars and on the last day she took herself up and along the steep climb into town, passed the stalls that spilled over the narrow road, laden with fruit, crafts, jewellery, woollen shawls and hats. Mr Gajender Sason caught up with her near the top, where, not for the first time, a family wanted her included in their photo. He told her all about herself by looking in her eyes, or so he said. He wasn't far wrong. He handed her his card. Meet, Experience & Feel Real India. Like many he was a shrewd business man.

On her way back, a monkey dropped from the trees onto a car roof, setting off the alarm, frightening itself; the monkey sprung in one leap across the road to scamper up to the high branches of the next tree then along the telephone wire. Irritatingly, The Little Red Monkey song played over and over in her head.

The Kuoni itinerary described it as a day at leisure. And it was – a lie in – a late breakfast – a read by the pool – 'finding yourself' tinkling mood music, almost feeling that she could take up the Lotus position and start chanting – a swim – cold – take your breath away cold – 3pm – time for lunch – biryani and a gin and tonic. Evenings were spent like others, drinking cups of black tea, reading, catching up with the news, watching the cricket offerings on Star Cricket, taking in the view that changed so suddenly in Shimla, heavy rainy skies had settled and in the distance there was thunder. Like wet chips spluttering in hot oil, the rain beat down on the corrugated tin roofs. As a rule, she didn't drink gin and tonic but decided that it would be her preferred drink when she reached Shimla as she could imagine the colonials sitting back on their verandas indulging in small talk, cursing the wretched heat, sweating and swotting flies, instead and though not usually a fan of Coke, she drank it. Embracing the Indian cuisine at every meal she remembered asking Sarog, who made the most divine samosas, long before the holiday was even thought about what people ate for breakfast as she could not picture an array of cereals being offered before the children went to school. She implied that it was left-overs. The 'Indian' breakfast in the hotels did not resemble left overs. She had a little spoonful of this and a little spoonful of that and all manner of different breads to dip and mop.

On the last day they were delivered safely to the airport. Browsing in the airport shops with excess rupees burning a hole in her little cotton purse, as they were of no value at home, she bought a scarf for herself and joss sticks packed in natural raffia bags and soap for each of her sons. Gift wrapped, they read like wine labels, each having a different mood. They were made from ancient recipes, full of character and spicy charm, with citrus undertones, subtle aromas, evocative fragrances and notes to warm your spirits, with a deeply comforting embrace, made of Himalayan Cedar, Exotic Lotus and Kashmiri Saffron.

After the uncomfortable, cramped outbound flight, she thankfully had a window seat and apart from glancing at the route home on her husband's TV screen and the distraction of the in-flight mini-meals that appeared at regular intervals she looked out of the window on her left for most of the four thousand miles home. The route took them over Pakistan, Afghanistan, Turkmenistan and Uzbekistan and from 36,000ft she could clearly see neat carpets of green and gold and furrowed brown, rugged dry escarpments, high remote wildernesses, winding roads and lazy rivers. The clouds stamped their muddy paw prints on the tidy earth. She did not see the sniper or the soldier killed in a grenade blast or tanks on manoeuvers raising clouds of dust to scroll across the ground. Passing over Kabul it looked peaceful. There were no signs of war, just as there had been no signs of poverty as they returned to Delhi in the dark. It was there none-the-less, insidious, lurking and menacing.

The patchwork land gave way to great banks of mounting cloud. It was amazing, vast piles of shovelled snow, deep gorging troughs, plunging ravines, churning whipped cream and towering pillars of meringue frothing and foaming like a bath of bubbles, carbonated drinks poured badly, spilling over, thin stippled sand and cushions and pillows and duvets of Polyester wadding laid lightly in the sky, swollen bladders and heaving lungs of gulping air, cauliflowers ballooning up, intensifying, doubling, trebling and quadrupling, caustic soda fizzing, fleecy soft cotton wool balls, the airiest, lightest soufflés blousing into the immense infinity.

3

By and large it felt that the whole country had settled somewhere to watch the match, like the sparrows all had gone quiet, a predator in the midst. England was playing Ukraine. Which team did her husband support? Where did his loyalties lie?

There was nothing lovelier than home-grown produce. Digging the first new potatoes was a memorable day, one noted in her husband's diary. From the middle of June they feasted on dreamy new potatoes, their filmy transparent skins, as fine as gossamer, simply 'melted in the mouth', there was no taste like it, add to that some raw onion and a couple of tablespoons of mayonnaise, mmm, heaven. Peas dripped from the hazel twig supports, broad beans nestled in their pods, protected in their fleecy beds. These were mainly shelled, blanched and frozen. She sat on her faded blue deck chair with her legs apart, the grass box between her feet for the pods and her mixing bowl clenched between her knees to collect the peas and beans. From Easter there had been a steady supply of lettuces and the fashionable mixed leaves. Last year she decided to have salads only in season, which meant there was no need to shop for tasteless icebergs and little gems thick with core. Green fringes of carrots filled the containers along with the tight furled leaves of spring onions. The damp 'Scottish' weather had been perfect for the abundant crop of raspberries, picked twice daily and made into flans and meringues and muffins. Then along came the beans. Like the peas, once they got going they dripped crisp and green in clusters, long and straight. Even eating them every day did not curtail the supply, the excess, like the peas and broad beans, was sliced, blanched and frozen.

She called it the birthday weekend, even though both birthdays fell either side of the weekend. It was like an event, on a par with Christmas and indeed it was special.

Inspired by a Moroccan holiday she had a whole tagine of recipes to draw from, and for the first meal she made the aptly named Moroccan chicken. All day the chicken marinated in a vat of spices; the fierce last minute frying brought on a coughing fit to anyone who drew breath in the kitchen, only to be cooled with handfuls of mint and wedges of orange. This she served with roasted vegetable couscous, disguising vegetables like aubergine and mushrooms that were usually left by someone round the edge of the plate. Usually, lack of time did not allow her to faff about, but having the time she made individual chocolate up and over puddings instead of a big family version with a statutory spoonful of extra-thick cream.

She could not spell what she made on Friday. It was Ukrainian food, the food that her mother-in-law (Nanny) used to make on special occasions, simple peasant food that took all day to prepare. It started first thing in the morning, levering cabbage leaves, without tearing them from the cabbage, carefully paring the coarse spine from each leaf and blanching them. Then she sliced, diced and fried an onion and cooked a pan of rice, Nanny had always stipulated pudding rice as there was a stickiness about it. Combining the rice and onion and, surprisingly, a squeeze of tomato sauce. Unavailable in her country, Nanny must have found tomato sauce a very handy addition. She spooned the mixture onto each leaf, carefully rolling them up and placing them closely together in an oven proof dish. Next, she made three quantities of dough with flour and milk and a pinch of salt, wrapping each in cling film so that it didn't dry out. She peeled and cooked a pan of potatoes; when they were ready her husband was on hand to mash.. She was the first to admit that mashing was not her forte. When the potato was cool, she rolled out the pastry really thin and cut circles. Here she felt bad because Nanny rolled the dough into a sausage shape and cut the length of dough into perfect humbug shapes and then rolled each piece individually into a perfect circle, filling each circle with a teaspoon of potato and sealing the edges with her thumb and forefinger. It was tedious and exacting and took forever and had to be done standing. As each was shaped it was lovingly placed on a clean tea towel and then covered with another. Before serving they were submerged in a pan of boiling water. She remembered going into Nanny's kitchen, condensation pouring from the walls, the mirror a fog. Sour cream accompanied the food along with gherkins and pork. She laid the table with Nanny's cloth. With a little bit of adaptation she was coming close to mastering the recipes because like Nanny's, however many she made there were never enough. Pudding – a chocolate almond torte – was thankfully made the previous day.

The big birthday dinner was on Saturday. It was a Chinese meal, a delicious medley of favourites, shapes and tastes; pork balls, mini Thai fish cakes, chicken satay, spring rolls, stir-fry vegetables, noodles and sweet and sour sauce, served in her largest dishes, for everyone to help themselves. The pièce de résistance had to be the raspberry pavlova. There was something hugely satisfying about preparing a meal for her family. As soon as the date was fixed, the expectation was there and she had to rise to the challenge, planning and shopping and cooking in advance, nothing was too much trouble. The food was the reason to sit down all together. While the event sometimes went on for hours, some would go out and come back later to find everyone still at the table where they had left them. Then the percolator went on and the cheese would come out. Everyone just sat around, or hung themselves over the arm of the settee while the dishwasher was filled until it groaned.

It was the fashion to steam. Although steaming was simple, she wasn't good at it, and more often than not vegetables were overcooked because she had not paid enough attention. With the present of a steamer came a boxed set of recipe cards, the kedgeree card immediately caught her eye and for quite some time had found its way to being a book mark in one of her well-thumbed books. She would make it for breakfast the next day. She used the recipe but the steamer was nowhere to be seen.

The birthday weekend ended with paella, which compared to all the other meals was almost incidental, made and served in one big pan with salad and garlic bread and morsels of left-over puddings at the kitchen table.

A recipe for a zesty lemon cordial caught her attention in a Saturday supplement. Basically, requiring lemons, sugar and water, not dissimilar to her mother's tangy thirst quenching recipe, but with an added twist, a handful of mint, she set to, grating the zest from the six lemons, squeezing the juice and adding the other ingredients; she brought the pan to the boil, simmered for ten minutes and allowed it to cool before straining. It was intensely refreshing with a keen, sharp kick; it reminded her of childhood summers, but it didn't leave the palate furred-up like shop-bought squashes – not that she bought them.

Seeing Michelle's face again, her warm smile and dancing eyes made the effort all worthwhile. Admittedly she had been undecided about going. It was a journey that required more thought and one that was not familiar. But she said that she would go and did not want to let her down. She was, after all, genuinely interested and believed in her friend's work. In the clinging heat of India she had enjoyed listening to her enthusiasm and admired her spirit and her passion and understood the 're-discovered' creative energy that had laid low for twenty years. Returning to learn was never easy.

Surprisingly, the journey was effortless. The platform was busy with commuters, a mixture of suits shirt sleeves and two brave girls wearing sleeveless summer dresses, goose bumps dotted their ample upper arms. Having come from somewhere else there were few seats available, but finding one she sat down next to a young man wearing jeans, Converse trainers and a pinkish coloured zipped up hoodie. Breathing deeply and clearly asleep his arms were folded across his chest and even when his phone rang, he merely shuffled and turned towards the window. After the initial burst of getting seated, no one spoke. Instead, people were engrossed in their laptops, their phones, their ipods and their e-books. There was the random sneeze, the shuffle of newspapers, and the occasional ring tone, and apart from a little rattle that didn't give up, the train slipped quietly along, a far cry from the clattering train from Kalka to Dehli. The countryside passed in a blur, rails and overhead cables merged and divided. Outside it was raining and she hoped not to regret leaving the umbrella in the car. Remembering St Pancras as a cold, draughty dump of a station, it had been transformed to a sparkling mall of glitzy shops and swishy cafes. She boarded the high speed train to Ashford, via Stratford International, whenever has Stratford been 'International' and Ebbsfleet International, that sounded like an immigration detention centre, then Ashford International. Under a crumpled sky the train disappeared into tunnels only to burst out moments later into the pale grey dampness, passed the QE2 Bridge, heavy with standing traffic, slick and efficient, passed inky woods and ponds and embankments of wavering grasses or showers of ox-eye daisies, poppies and buttercups, over the Medway and into lush green Kent.

It was an excellent show, bursting with promise, everyone pumped and enthusiastic, a culmination of dedicated hard work. Her friend's work was daring and risky but that only added to its appeal. A lift back to the station and a big hug brought their reunion to a close until they met again.

Her son would have called, the man sitting opposite, a dick. Her husband would have called him a tosser. Obviously smug and pleased with his own performance he was on his phone longing to gloat over a competitor's misfortune. He was loose tongued, name dropping, and he let all five people in the carriage on the way back through the especially named for the 2012 Olympics, International stations, know that he had managed the God dammed hill. He didn't seem to know however, where he was in relation to where he had been. His bike tyres were as sharp as his saddle, and he wore Shimano shoes that clicked into his pedals, and tight Lycra shorts with a much needed padded arse. He looked the part.

Still the rain spluttered. The Shard was hidden in festering cloud and the landmark buildings of Canary Wharf, where her latest book was pending, were barely visible. Catching the Corby train at four o'clock, still no-one spoke.

Very occasionally she went fishing with her husband. While he set up his rods and baited-up she took in her immediate surroundings. She sat on a fat wedge of foam on a little fold-up chair in a pleasant grassy glade. Nearby and opposite, the willows breathed, rhythmically pitching in the wind, scattering the lightest of seeds that eventually drifted to land and collected on a mat of floating weedy scum.

Nourished with goose droppings and sheep shit, the tousled grass was dense and thick with the ferny leaves of silverweed, dotted with solitary yellow flowers, white clover, tough stalks of plantain and ryegrass. Scattered feathers indicated an untimely death for a wood pigeon. Along the bank in front of her, amid the leaning reeds and sedges yellow flags stood to attention. The pin-thin dancing turquoise damselflies flaunted and flitted dizzily above the continually changing surface of the lake. The open water assumed the view above it, silvery ruffles mirrored the racing clouds and around the edges, where the trees hung over, the reflection was dark and foreboding. Where the water was placid, swirls and dimples broke the surface.

The splashing fracas of marauding Canadian geese earlier had been resolved and they proceeded in a sedate procession across the lake. In the margins a moorhen dabbled amongst the tangle of branches that dipped into the water, bathing and preening. In love, swans courted. Her husband hissed at them when they came too close to his line. He was not a lover of swans.

Above, heaving shoulders of cloud moved through, overtaking and separating, fizzling out and breaking every now and then to reveal warm pockets of blue sky. A buzzard mewed. A green woodpecker laughed, a heron banked and the house martins swooped and dipped in the water. Like a load of sheep, a large flock of resident sheep, their fleeces sheered to the quick, tunelessly baaed and bleated their way round the lake. She read her book in the swirling wind. It would have been idyllic but for the perpetual background noise of the roaring motorway traffic.

Saturday 23rd June. It was over a month since she had walked and settling back into the routine was hard. Her walk had changed. A mesmerising sea of sweeping grasses leaned and swayed in the wind. A faded lacy veil, the colour of grated nutmeg and drinking chocolate mingled with mauves and grey, rippled and waved, shimmered and caught the light and the shadows as the scurrying cloud swept through. The grasses were twice the height and from a distance, people walking their dogs were submerged and their dogs nowhere to be seen. Paths were less defined but as wet as ever, squelching and streaming from the overnight deluge. Her forging pace did not lessen and she could hear her boots scuffing through the grass and slopping in the wet. Here and there handsome musk thistles thrived and the rusty docks and sorrels had sprung up. In the hedges, dog roses and elderflower had replaced the May blossom. Remembering when she could only take a hasty glimpse over the school field, longing to be in the fresh air instead of the sweltering pot-boiling conditions of her classroom, especially lesson six on a Thursday afternoon when sweat trickling down her back. Where was the romantic view of lazily sitting on the scattered benches, reading and writing? Where were those balmy summer days? Where were the benches? Most were completely obscured in the long grass. Had she not seen them in April she would not have known they were there. An eager collie stopped and looked at her. Saying good morning to its owner was a mistake. The entrance to the next field was thick with slippery mud and further on the view between the trees had changed, the yellow fields had gone, the trees had filled between the gaps. The river was brown and swirling, silver where the sun flirted in the shifting light. The voice recorder was no longer in her bag, but held loosely in her hand, ready.

Listening to her uneven voice afterwards, she sounded tense, a timid blubbering wreck, almost tearful, panting for breath and her feet going at such a pace stumbling along, scuffling through the grass or if it was wet, squelching. When it was wet and blustery a bold dull thud reverberated and she sensed her sniffing and the need to blow her nose. When she became frustrated with the incessant wet ground she moaned to herself like her mother. She could barely make out what she said and had to hold the voice recorder close to her ear. It was pathetic and not at all like she was and she didn't like the whiney sound or the dictatorial tone of her voice. She wished her voice was deeper, huskier, drier. Thankfully no one else heard the recordings and they were deleted as soon as they were transferred into notes.

Much more interesting to hear again were the background noises, that of the wind, which even on a breezy day was grossly exaggerated, sounding ferocious, like a tarpaulin free of its lashings or an escaping sail flapping or the rain draining from a leaky gutter or the birds twittering or calling shrilly or the mallards quacking incessantly and the faint whistle of her jeans as her knees rubbed together or the low squeak of her sleeves rubbing against the sides of her waxy jacket. She tried talking softly and sweetly into the voice recorder, without success. Sometimes other people's voices could be heard or the whine of the metal gates opening and closing.

"Who are you talking to?" He asked from downstairs.

"Nobody." She called back.

"I could hear you talking." He insisted.

"That's just the voice recorder." She replied.

Hoping to see a velvet bat, she took her coffee outside. In the advancing umbra the garden quietly closed in. Frogs made their way to the black slip of pond, scrambling over the net to plop into the water. Leaning back in her deck chair she watched the sky. It was the first summer evening not to be pelting rain or blowing a gale. She remembered thirty three years ago, bringing her precious son home at last from hospital and feeling totally inadequate. Day and night he slept in snatches, crying and shrieking until he had no breath. He threw up his feed. After being institutionalized for a fortnight, the isolation of home was a terrible shock. She couldn't bear to hear his rasping cries setting her on edge and picked him up to comfort him. When her husband came in from work, he would cuddle him and proudly walk around the garden, along the chain link fence that separated the new houses from theirs and along the path by the washing line, a nappy flung over his shoulder, gently rubbing his exquisitely soft downy back in soothing circles. Subsequent babies were never so demanding. In those few moments she thought as she sat there, without noticing, time was slipping by. Again, the following evening she sat in the warped half-light, breathing the lingering heady scent of the philadelphus, its boughs heavy with blossom and listing badly, staring and scanning the acres of sky, hoping to see a glimpse of a bat. Looking on, half a fuzzy orange moon gave no light. If there was a bat she would know by its sudden quick movements. Silently, just after ten when the birds had stopped twittering, they dropped from their daytime retreats to feed on the moths at a daring, darting speed.

In a sudden squall the lettuce just took off and left the plate, to roll around gathering dirt along with the fallen petals snatched from the nearby clematis and the dying leaves whipped-up from the undergrowth. It was rarely so warm thus the reason for eating al fresco and the wind rarely so fierce, warm and fierce, relentlessly bending and pushing the garden about. The trees writhed and pitched throwing themselves at the mercy of the elements. Hastily she clamped a naan bread on top to anchor the escaping lettuce.

Another lettuce incident occurred when the old kitchen was being gouged out. Again they were eating in the garden and it was lunch time. The lettuce had been well washed but at the last minute she had cut a handful of leaves and mixed them through. Fortunately her husband declined the salad because he didn't want the dressing alternative to salad cream. Calmly arching his hairy back the greenest of caterpillars more than an inch long walked out from the jungle of leaves and around the edge of her plate. She said nothing, didn't even flinch, with a quick flick he was returned to the herbaceous border to live another day and she continued, albeit reluctantly, with her salad.

Friday 29th June. After walking several miles in the driving wind the zesty ice cold Pimms was just what was needed, keen and sharp it quenched their thirst and the three friends settled into a balmy alcohol-induced afternoon, catching-up, comfortable in each other's company, sharing the gossip and their thoughts, off-loading, eating and sipping in between. All of which came to a sudden finish when a phone call intruded. Bloody phones. Feeling a little deflated at the abrupt end to the soiree she and her friend took themselves to their local. Walking up to the bar they said hello to all and sundry. Attentive as always Jill leaned over the bar. "I've seen you both before but never together." It sounded like a challenge as though their reputation of being notorious drinkers preceded them and to watch this space. "Now what can I get you?" A bottle of Pinot Grigio along with two glasses was placed on the bar and dutifully enjoyed and the next bottle was ordered and opened and she thought when their mouths had lost their shape and the words came out all wrong and their brains took more than a second to react that she was glad that the early drinkers were not there to see them when they stumbled out nearly three hours later. The early sun fell hotly on the fading lining of the curtains and even with her eyes shut a blinding shard of light slashed like a glinting sword through the gap between them and skewered her head to the pillow. She was sedated for twelve hours and by midday wine still coursed through her veins instead of blood. Meeting up did not always end in a drunken stupor. Sometimes they took tea in the afternoon.

She was not averse to tea and once at The Tea Palace near Portobello Road had the most expensive, although not the most expensive cup of tea ever, called Russian Caravan, chosen from many as it conjured an image of fur hats and gypsies and the haunting sound of the balalaika, it was grossly overpriced. Lovely breakfasting atmosphere – clinking china cups and saucers, linen cloths, crinkling broadsheets – but grossly overpriced.

4

2nd July 2012. It could have been October, it was dreich and drizzly, windy and not that warm. It was the 2nd of July 2012. The grasses had lost their appetite. Laden and soaked with rain they leaned heavily and low in the wind, their heads nodded but they looked tired and lacked lustre. Without sun they did not sparkle. Last week she had seen them in all their glory. For several days the greedy wind had ripped through flattening them like a poor harvest. It was a cheerless sight.

And then she came across the remnants of a fire, a fairly extensive fire, broadcast over the path where the path led towards the river. The scattered fluttering ash had stuck in the rain. Pages ripped from books and torn from staples had been ceremoniously and deliberately burnt to celebrate the end of an era. Half charred some had escaped the leaping inferno to lodge in the long grass, littering the Common. Without touching them she deftly leaned in and over in order to have a look and find a link to the arsonists. Strewn about were handwritten English notes and essays, tables on graph paper and physics pages about electricity. Was it a gesture of defiance, openly mocking their education, their teachers, their parents and their own future, or were the students participating in an ancient pagan ritual, singing and dancing in thanks that the exams were over? 'School's out forever.' Could they not have just put it all in a pink recycling sack and gone to the pub? What a waste. It tried to rain. Like a little coloured truncheon her umbrella dangled from her wrist.

Thursday 5th July. On Wednesday night she weighed out ingredients ready to make raspberry muffins. Leaving them to cool on Thursday morning she put on her boots and went out.

It was warm and sunny. Pounding across the Common her jumper was soon off and tethered round her waist. It was glorious. Yellow swathes of ladies bedstraw and florets of yarrow had inched through the grasses. Dew sparkled like sequins in the glittering sunlight. The day made her feel brave and impulsive and she had decided to walk the circular walk. The confines of the narrow lane closed around her as it climbed away. There was a sour tang of undergrowth and a dense smell of musty vegetation of decaying leaf matter and roots. It was airless. Flies buzzed. The close-knit branches reached and entwined across the path, the cow parsley had gone to seed and bent over, brambles clawed at her jeans. Her boots slapped through the mud. Not one to like the feeling of being enclosed she was glad to be away from the lurching shadows and back in the open, reaching the small lakes where in recent years gravel had been extracted. Here the motorway crossed the flood plain. Contentedly cattle grazed. Above them traffic pounded along. Turning, she crossed the river towards the farm away from the reverberating noise. Barking, a Labrador and a terrier rushed up to check her out. Crossing the farmyard a curl of air brought with it the whiff of bacon. The narrow track of ploughed fallow land that led away from the farm was barely visible, overgrown with redleg. Either side, coarse and wet spent oil seed rape as high as her shoulders, was waiting to be harvested. She pushed her way through and emerged at the other end, her socks and jeans soaked. The walk, indicated on the gate posts with yellow arrowed discs, had to her reached its furthest point and it was time to make her way back. There were no signs that anyone had done the walk for a while, the wooden gate was bound tightly with bindweed and goose-grass and required a hefty push to open it wide enough for her to squeeze through. Spotted with poppies, a broad grassy path hemmed in the wheat field and here and there scentless mayweed and red sandwort spurrey scattered through the verges. The hedges sheltered and it was warm, not a breath of wind. Butterflies flitted and fluttered and the warming sun soon blotted her jeans dry. Before leaving she had left a note on the kitchen table, 'gone to get milk' and in passing back through the town on her way home, she called in to the Co-op to get some.

It was the annual carnival. People lined the route expectantly craning their necks in anticipation. Although not cold, the unsettled weather meant that few were without umbrellas, folded in their hands. The police van came through first, hazard lights blazing, followed by the swing of kilts and the evocative sound of a pipe band. Royalty was this year's theme and every float was adorned with union jack bunting looped and fluttering. The continuing national events of 2012 justified the reason for high streets up and down the land to be draped with flags. Like God, national pride was fairly low on the agenda and thinly spread. Too many things had made her think in this way. Being sceptical, she did not especially become involved in patriotic street parties and sport, nor the 'in your face media', it wasn't that she was a sourpuss, somehow it seemed false when most people in the road barely said good morning. However, she was happy enough to stand with her bag of change for the charity buckets and admire the effort that went into the royal scenes that passed before her. Music blared and everyone was in good spirits.

Reading books took up too much time and as a novel progressed so she found herself compelled, desperate to finish as though her life depended on it, picking it up more and more often, glutinously eating her way through it, a surrogate for anything else, she read ferociously longing to know the outcome, which often, in her opinion, could be disappointing.

When reading, she felt at times that she had the look of her mother about her, hunched over her book, the glasses perched, never quite straight on her nose, peering through them at the words on the page. She seemed to remember her mother holding her book up with one hand, reading until her eyes tired and closed, until her arm wearied and dropped to her lap, her head drooping forward as she fell asleep. Sleeping for only a minute or two, her mother would give a sudden involuntary lurch and spring to life again, shuffle in her seat, re-cross her legs and resume reading as though she had never left off. There was no one to see her. If she was sitting in the sitting room on a comfy chair, reading had that effect on her too. Like some people do not make charity shop purchases, some people would not borrow books from a library, preferring instead to buy new books, not liking the fact that library books had been in other people's hands and houses, their cars and bags, on journeys to work or on holidays abroad. It was true that best sellers and popular titles were well thumbed and tinged brown with being picked up and put down so many times. With so much handling sometimes small cracks appeared along the edges of the clammy polythene covers scratching and snagging threads. Corners were tired and curled. Careless drips of wine or coffee had caused pages to pucker or thunder flies had met an untimely death or food accidently spilt had stained, sometimes leaving gritty indents. In her most recent read crushed within the pages were dots of something berry red then further on there was a splatter of turmeric smeared. Even she was guilty of a splodge of digestive biscuit that had failed to make it from her cup of tea to her mouth, and it was nearly impossible to keep a paperback pristine on a Mediterranean beach, the pages just broke away from the spine in the simmering heat. A lengthy doorstep of a book virtually disintegrated and she apologized profusely when she returned it to the library and could see the book on the 50p trolley wedging the door open. Instead of using a bookmark, readers had marked their places with triangular folds in the corners. Yes, there was a grubbiness about them.

She used to borrow several books at once, but the allotted lending time changed from four weeks to three, barely enough time for her to read one. She was not what she called a fast reader. However arduous she was not one to skim or scan but gave every word her utmost attention. And she read a book until the bitter end, even though it was maybe not her cup of tea or it was plainly boring, as though it had been dealt as a punishment and she wasn't allowed to leave the table until her plate was clean.

Occasionally, while reading she found that other authors' novels were seasoned with the same similes and peppered with the same metaphors. People using words interspersed in their writing in the same way as her was disconcerting, and it was disturbing that people might think that she was guilty of plagiarizing which she knew to be a cardinal sin. And yet, words were not exclusively theirs, not unlike two guests wearing identical outfits at a wedding. It was bound to happen. In the throes of her fourth novel, she constantly found herself checking her own titles for such discrepancies.

Her appetite for reading increased hugely when she no longer worked and instead of only reading in the holidays it was every day. Even so, finishing within three weeks was rarely achieved, often calling the library at the eleventh hour to renew the book to avoid paying the fine. It was rare, but once she devoured a whole book in one sitting, leaving it splayed when she had to stop and eat or see to food. The entire book was starved of punctuation, with little more than full stops and commas. She didn't skip any part of it or slide her eyes over the page. It was gripping and she was rapt. Or maybe she read a book quickly because it was thin. However, thinking that she could ever remember all the stories she read was impossible and as soon as the next book was started they were quickly forgotten. A book was a new found friend and it was reliable, always there ready to pick up or put down at a moment's notice, there when she needed to seek shelter from a storm. Reading filled long spaces of empty time and because of its handy size a book could go anywhere, she could sit in the garden anchoring the fluttering pages with her thumbs, she read when the TV offered nothing but sport, she read when waiting for pots to boil or in the car or when it was raining. She rarely read in bed. If she lay down her glasses felt askew, as though she might snap the arm or she held the book too close and the words were out of focus and if she held it further away her arms ached. In the winter her warm breath puffed into the shivering cold air. In the summer, the windows were open and the moths attracted by the light, would flit frantically around, dicing with death between the light bulb and the shade. While there was a moth in the room she couldn't settle, even if it went to ground she would have to get up and find it, gather it up in a cloth and throw it back outside.

More often than not she generally chose a book by its cover, drawn in by the graphics, the colours, the layout or the scrawled title. However they didn't always hit the mark. Increasingly feeling irritated by the author depicting the characters as being affluent, with families having a nanny or children sent away to school, speaking like Margot on The Good Life or the 'frightfully, frightfully' plummy voices portrayed on the radio programme The Archers. How many meals did they take at Manderlay? Over the years she had met thousands of children and their families and they simply did not come across like that.

Paradoxically although it freed up her invaded time again, on completing a book she felt at a loss. Used to the characters she felt that she got to know them personally and suddenly her relationship with them had come to an abrupt end. It was time to get to the library to choose another book. There were times when one after the other she read the world's best sellers, One Day followed by The Slap, followed by The Help which just happened to be on the swivel shelf waiting to be picked up. That was what was good about the library, years later, when almost forgotten, random books reappeared and were given a new lease of life.

Instead of stamping the return date with a little date marker she received a receipt and even though she had book marks and postcards she used it as a book mark and a reminder of the due date. On the back of each she planned to jot a few notes.

There on the swivel shelf was her book. Picking it up, she opened it. The sheet with all the local Library telephone numbers was stuck on the front page and on the next was the library stamp with the word donation written by hand. It was wrapped of course in a plastic sleeve. Flicking through it she glanced at what she had written and she wanted to say to the man sitting near the window. "I wrote this. You should read it."

She was standing, absently turning the swivel bookcase and was aware of another woman, already holding a book and needing another, also scanning the titles. Again her eyes fell on her own book. "What about reading this? She said, removing it smartly and presenting it to her. "I wrote it." She enthused. The woman was approachable and keen to try new authors turning it over to read the blurb on the back.

To sit with a book – her legs up on the settee and covered with a blanket, the windows blurry with streaming rain was an idle luxury that once she could only dream of doing. And yet paradoxically she wanted and enjoyed having the choice but it hit a nerve, at the same time she was fearful of becoming like her mother. It was what her mother did. All the time she would sit and read and drowse. She did not want that for herself, preferring most of the time to luxuriate in the guilty pleasure waiting for the potatoes to boil or the washing to finish so that she could hang it out sitting on a hard kitchen chair.

She had finished her much acclaimed book, a reasonable enough story but for her it did not live up to or portray the untold horror that would have undoubtedly existed. Usually, once started she devoured the pages, turning them rapidly, but she had found the book slow going. The whole book was well researched and included maps and old photos. Its historical content was interesting, allowing her in to see the chiaroscuro and the Prologue and the Epilogue came close to her expectations, but overall it was sterile, too wholesome, like a Sunday evening period soap drama. It lacked vitriol and was not convincing, with too much of the present written into the past. It was too clean, too, too perfect. It didn't have an edge to get your teeth into. It could have been an emotional story, but it didn't jolt her tears or leave her longing. However the book reviews raved about it and it featured in the top-ten paperbacks for weeks. What did she know? Her next book was the exact opposite, a page turner. She didn't put it down. Reading voraciously it was returned to the library within days. It was what she liked about the words, earthy and basic, journeying into people's minds, authentic, accurate and convincing. Reading nourished. It opened up another way of looking at landscapes and journeys. It was private. From wherever she was she could day dream and escape from the here and now, go back in time, go somewhere else, be someone else.

It was unlikely that she would ever be a guest on Desert Island Discs, but if she was, she would choose the complete works of Charles Dickens. It was her intention to start reading what were called the classics. At school of course she had been force-fed Chaucer, Jane Austin and Shakespeare and the fact that they needed great explanations and copious notes put her off. She worried also about the language and that it wasn't cool to be seen reading them. It was her love of the 1948 black and white version of Oliver Twist that decided her first author. At the library, although sometimes moved around, the classics were easily located, either at the far end by the window, or, as a reminder to readers that they still existed, by the front desk. They of course had always been there to read in her lifetime as were places in Britain that she promised to visit and films that she had missed and intended to see when she had the time. For a while, her impatience when younger, and then the lack of time when working, the reading of books eluded her.

She felt that there had to be something about the classics that set them apart. Many had endured for decades. Indeed there were things. It might be a fairly straightforward story but the authors and writers of the day wrote vividly. Strewn in rich detail, everything minutely described, the characters intricately woven, and the atmosphere realistic.

The author might only know of his or her immediate vicinity or social class, what they themselves had experienced and what people did from day to day. There would have been a few paintings or early photographs to reference and they were probably entirely reliant on what they knew, unlike today, bombarded as they are with television, films, books, magazines and the internet. Sometimes she felt that the authors today dispensed with the familiar with the presumption that the reader could see the shadows in the dimly lit street, the litter swirling in the wind, the moon glancing now and then and so didn't need reminding. Desperate to keep up the momentum the story hurries on. It cannot be assumed that the reader will envisage the pile of dishes on the side, the uncombed hair, the everyday and the ordinary which are ever present in any time. How can contentment or atmosphere be described without reference to these things?

The slower pace of those times was reflected in the time it took to read them. There was so much social history to be learnt, scenes to imagine. For her, the newly founded classics justly deserved the long time spent reading them, justifying the time spent writing them. After all, she had all the time in the world, well the next thirty years.

She began to read Great Expectations and indeed it did take longer to read and was renewed several times. The slow read however did not lessen the enjoyment. Unlike contemporary novels this did not seem to matter as it would always be there. Sometimes she needed to re-read to make sure she fully understood. She loved the absorbing narrative, life in the city so richly described, likening it to what she knew, Mr Dickens's keen eye, his dry sense of humour and at times puzzling satire, becoming fond of the characters and their quirky ways, how Herbert and Handel dealt with their debts at Bernard's Inn. Despite her earlier criticism of explanations needed about the text, she was more than thankful to refer to the 'explanatory notes' at the back, translating the text as though it was a foreign language.

She was frozen with indecision about the oven and it was beginning to annoy. The 'all singing all dancing' 'in your face' range cookers were all the fashion, gleaming and distracting, stealing the show whenever someone different walked into the kitchen. She really didn't want to enter into long conversations about its appearance, running their fingers along the chrome trim or to hear the lilt of envy. For God's sake it was just something to cook on/in. Long ago she had always liked the idea of stoking the Aga, huddling around it to keep warm, endlessly simmering. Homely and quaint. Instead, she wanted slim and sleek, easy to clean and however splashed with food, it still had to look good. Whatever she decided had to be functional and every bit as good as her present arrangement and as long lasting. She had been to all the stores, checked on-line, looked in brochures and bored people with oven chat. Despite the huge, bewildering choice, she was hard to please, most she ruled out immediately, nothing was quite what she wanted. Basically the depths of the double ovens were too small, and while the ordinary oven was a good size it doubled as a grill and that could be inconvenient. In the specification it talked about the capacity in litres. It was misleading and confusing. She wanted to know if she could fit a 5lb chicken and a tray of roast potatoes. Those descriptions were not written by anyone who cooked. Armed with the depth of her largest crock-pot she measured the insides of the ovens and decided in the end, although extravagant, to have two separate ovens to cover all eventualities. At the same time did she really need two ovens? Decisions, decisions, although not a weekly occurrence she went backwards and forwards several times before making one, either to justify the need or to check on the forever changing offers. Almost paralyzed with indecisiveness, in the end she reverted to her original choice, knowing that she would never again cook a 12lb turkey; it was probably unlikely anyway. The deal was done. Monday 9th of July Jason ordered the hob, the oven and a dishwasher.

Sunday 15th July. Sunny days were in short supply. Making the most of the high bright sky on St Swithan's Day she reversed the walk she had done ten days before. Following round the undulating field she could see already that despite the sunless days the wheat was already tinged with a hint of change. Within weeks it would be a swathe of pale swaying prairie. There was always a feeling of romantic nostalgia, a little bit of a longing at the timeless sight of ripening crops or bales of straw and fields of stubble. The path looked disturbed, as though two people had trampled the circular walk, sometimes fizzling out only to reappear again further on.

Caught in the sunlight, needles of blue damsel flies hovered in the wet grass and a new rash of poppies peppered the edges. Above, the trees gently hissed like pebbles dragged along the beach in the running tide. At the first farm it was quiet, the barn doors shuttered and the gates closed. At the furthest point she turned into the green ribbon of redleg, flattened and a little more defined and thankfully not wet, that ran between the oil seed rape towards the second farm where she was seen off by the barking dogs.

As she neared she could see that the cows were well distributed, some just ambling along eating the grass, others with their calves beside them, turning to look at her as she stepped into their field. Some mooed urgently, warning. Not taking her big brown eyes from her, one increased her pace putting herself between the intruder and her calf. Feeling uneasy she back tracked a short way and took the more isolated farm track that led under the motorway.

Under the thundering traffic it was eerily dark. Underfoot it was wet and slippery. Looming on her left was a graveyard of farm machinery, vague grey shapes of rusting hoppers and balers, feeding troughs and coops, decomposing and left to decay. Two years ago she had walked with her son on a dreary, damp November afternoon and it was he who was unnerved by the unfamiliar menacing shapes that emerged through the gloom. Being used to farms and not in the least intimidated by what she saw, she was able to say what the threatening almost torturous looking machinery was used for, which put his mind at rest to a certain degree. Walking alone however, the tension ramped-up. Apprehension moved over her face. The isolation made her feel nervous. Focusing on the dazzling brightness at the far end of the tunnel her pace quickened as did her heart. Not until she was out in the sunshine again did her pounding heart calm down. The detour was miles further and no longer part of the circular walk.

The need to get a paper took her to the local centre, passed the house and remembering little of where she used to live forty years ago. She could picture wall-papering the bathroom one evening when her husband was on the late shift, with a dark pre-pasted moody print. Running some water in the bath, she cut a length, soaked it and attached it to the wall. Unlike now when she could wield an axe with the best of them, in those days, unscrewing the bathroom cabinet would have been a man's domain. Not daring to remove it she papered round it and even now she can see the uncomfortable stamp of wall where the cabinet had been. She remembered the warm-air heating system and kneeling down beside the grill to dry her hair. It was about all it was good for. And when the tilt of the afternoon sun fell over the sitting room door it warped and wouldn't close. She remembered, when she had passed her driving test, though you wouldn't think she had, completely misjudging and missing the drive and driving instead straight across the grass, knocking the "For Sale" sign down. She still remembered the phone number; Goldcrest 612804. Mainly the house lacked character, indeed it was the reason for moving. Passing, the house itself was unchanged, almost neglected. Over the years nobody had added a porch or an extension or improved the two runs of concrete that served as a drive. Two straggly roses remained, her roses, "Teenager", were still there bordering the path in the tired front garden and in desperate need of pruning. At the time it was just about the only house for sale and certainly the only house they could afford. Built on the fringes of the development, the road not yet made and from the back bedroom window they had an uninterrupted view to the river. Since then a labyrinth of Culs-de-Sac, Closes, Drives, Walks, Avenues and Ways and hundreds and hundreds of houses had encroached and filled the view.

A warm golden glow filled the bedroom. The day started, as it often did with a bowl of blue sky and streaming sun. Not thinking it would last she went prepared for every eventuality. The night before she located her ruck-sack and proceeded to fill it with a banana and two satsumas for breakfast on the train, sunglasses and a sleeveless top in case it remained sunny, a warm cardigan in case it turned cold, an umbrella in case it rained, a pouch of blackcurrant juice in case she was suddenly thirsty, a disposable cup as she was not good at drinking from a bottle, nor did it suit her, a scrunchie in case she needed to control her hair and her all-important notebook. Arriving unnecessarily early at the station, she bought her ticket, returned to the car and sat listening to Radio 4 while she painted her nails, a job she always left to the last minute, there was never a good time. She had been glad to get up. A dream verging on terror between 6am and 6.45am left her feeling thick and tainted with malaise. Not until she had consumed her 'picked up at the station latte like thousands of others,' along with her banana. The continuing inclement weather had postponed her day trip to Brighton, she had become as bad as her husband, checking the forecast. The train from Bedford went straight there, no need to get off and change in London, it was so easy and she was anxious to go before the mad influx of tourists arrived for the Olympic Games. She loved being by the sea and was happy enough to hire a deck chair out of the wind, facing the sea and just stare at the view. Even the effortless journey was enjoyable. The embankments, densely overgrown, interspersed with flourishes of rose bay, willow herb, lacy traveller's joy and spikes of buddleia gave way to the changing skyline of outer London, in the distance, the steel arc at Wembley, slipping over the points, the outskirts of the city, plunging underground to gently glide into St Pancras International where nearly everyone got off. The train snaked in and out of the darkness. Above her, old Victorian brick buildings and dimples of bright sky, now and then quick glimpses of the river, the London Eye and a reflection of St Paul's in the open door. On her left, the Shard, starred with sunlight, speared the sky, glinting like a hologram, reflecting the chasing clouds it dwarfed the nearby buildings. Weaving cautiously through the city, overlooking the warren of Dickensian housing, the confusion of roofs and clustered chimneys, the train gradually picked up speed through the leafy suburbs of the commuter belt, the verges wild with bracken and into the rolling farmland of the Sussex countryside to almost plummet towards the sea, teetering on the edge of Brighton.

As soon as she stepped out of the station she had been targeted, a day tripper, singled out like an injured wildebeest, a victim. Before leaving she had checked the map for alternative activities, if need be, to the stony beach. Catching sight of the sea and hearing the plaintive cries of the gulls however, all those ideas were instantly forgotten and she walked straight down to Kings Road and crossed at the lights to walk the hurly-whirly length of the lower promenade, sampling the tasty morsels from the fish stalls, soft light crab and anchovies wrapped round a stuffed olive, the salty taste of the sea impaled on a stick. Once done with walking, she sought out fish and chips and sat down on one of the all-important stripy deck chairs scattered around in pairs. It was impossible to be out of the wind, but the sun was out and picking at her chips she arranged herself, carefully lifting the polystyrene tray to her lap. Magic. Within moments of being settled the gulls daringly swooped in on her and snatched the entire contents from her hands, one gull had her whole piece of fish, didn't even share it, and the chips, well, it was a feeding frenzy, all over in less than half a minute. In disbelief she looked on, standing up when it was all over to retrieve the napkin that had blown away in the commotion. Feeling deprived, she sat back and took in her surroundings, sipping at juice, instead, from the white plastic cup. The gusting wind powered onshore dissolving any sound from the nearby pier. The swell, whipped up by the wind sparkled throwing a great froth of spray onto the bank of shingle. White horses surfaced the distance. Yellow buoys bobbed. Fretting cloud heaped in, it felt chilly and she did not want to resurrect the cardigan from her bag. Instead, she walked briskly along the front and back towards the station, nipping into M&S to grab a sandwich. Looking out for gulls she settled into her seat and carefully tore along the perforated line. Until the monumental spire of The Shard came into view, she noticed little of the journey home.

Coming in from swimming she gathered the fliers from the mat in the hall. Amongst them was a letter. Still holding her bag she walked through the house and put the fliers in the recycling basket by the back door. With the bag still over her arm she opened the letter. The publisher's wanted her to send the complete manuscript. Wow. Over the next few days, even though it had been 'finished' for over a year she read it through and tweaked the odd word. There were discrepancies and glaring errors and it probably needed a complete overhaul but still she posted it off.

However, as soon as it was slipped under the glass shutter in the Post Office and placed in the sack leaning in the corner behind the counter to be collected later by Tom, out on his rounds, parked outside on the double yellow lines and taken, she assumed, to the sorting office, she had misgivings, picturing sentences that could be improved and what had she got to say that was interesting to read and the years of work and she didn't send it recorded delivery. Allowing the manuscript to enter the public domain suddenly made her feel protective about it. What was done was done. It was out of her control. Then what happened? Did it go in a large red lorry to London to be sorted again into area post codes, being handled through the night, thrown about, whisked away on a conveyor belt and pigeon-holed to be delivered the next day to the glitzy offices in Canary Wharf with lots of lipstick smiles and thank yous, or would it arrive late, on Saturday when there was no one there except the security guard, standing resolute, his hands behind his back staring out through the rain splattered smoked glass windows at the empty shadowy pavements? All these thoughts spread through her as she walked back home, too anxious even to book her trip to the sea side. The next day she made three changes to the manuscript. By mid-September she had made three more, nothing drastic, just words she preferred to the existing ones. An A4 envelope arrived and in it a letter and a contract to sign. It was the scariest thing. An email came in November with all the admin things to do for her new book. From the NASA website she printed out her favourite starry images and folded the pages in half to look like covers. Even though she read the information permitting the use of NASA Images, she wanted to see it in black and white. A reply from an email sent the previous August was returned in March, granting her permission to use 'Deep inside the Milky Way', followed by 'Have an outstanding day'.

Saturday 21ˢᵗ July. The sun was warm on her back. In step, her shadow stretched out ahead. It was perfectly still. Bluebottles buzzed. Like antlers, great clumps of rusting sorrel forged high and thick through the grasses. Underfoot it was very wet, in places ribbons of water streamed over the path, people had walked further away to avoid the marshy ground. It was the reason she hadn't walked across the Common for a while. Ahead of her an Alsatian, a large Alsatian carrying a red ball in its mouth was going to cross the path at exactly the same time as her. If she speeded up the dog might be agitated, she sensed herself slowing. So did the dog. It knew she was uneasy and stood scowling, watching her. Further round two girls on horseback sauntered, chatting and laughing. Swifts flirted with the ground. Nearing the Mill Street exit, a horse whinnied.

Due to their pets, it was rare that their special friends stayed overnight. After lunch under the shady pergola they went out on a nostalgic tour down memory lane, driving to where she and her friend used to live, retracing steps, meandering around the churchyard, renewing her family ties held dear, stopping by where her reception was held on that bright freezing cold March day in 1979, where drifting snow nearly brought her horse and carriage to a slippery stop then on passed the zoo to pick up a large order of acclaimed sausages. Dinner was timed for 8 30pm. They sat outside in the shrinking light till the early hours. She made a chicken curry served with an array of authentic side dishes and accompaniments, exacting recipes, not trialled before.

Returning to the garden for a long lazy breakfast, full English along with orange juice, pots of tea and coffee and a batch of freshly made chocolate and walnut muffins. Twenty four hours later it was time to leave. It came to an end too quickly.

Meeting up with her friends again it was a sober affair, coffee followed by soda and lime and lunch. Having enjoyed a week of their holidays her two friends were relaxed, with virtually no sign of their bitter grumbles. Knowing her fascination for the city, Mandy gave her a book, '1000 things to do in London for under £10'. Quickly flicking through, she was transported here there and everywhere. Dr Samuel Johnson said "When a man is tired of London, he is tired of life; for there is in London all that life can afford." She had never tired of London.

It was arranged that they met at eleven to walk along the Ouse nearer to its source, a gravelled riverside walk taking in meadows and the meandering flow. A tractor pulling a grass cutter worked its way towards the middle of the field, leaving in its wake clods of lush mown grass. The smell, a favourite for some hung in the air. On the bank fathers passed on their fishing expertise to their young sons and where the river formed a shallow bay, where a small boat could be launched, young children blue with cold and oblivious to the dangers, played and shrieked in the freezing water. Never lost for words, the three firm friends slipped into conversation, lunched and walked and stopped for tea in a sunny courtyard, finalising arrangements for the upcoming trip to Oxford.

It was an attractive mug, decorated with cricket memorabilia transfers. It was why it had been bought. It came packaged to avoid breakage. "I'll have my new cup." Her husband requested when she offered tea. While waiting for the kettle to boil, she dropped a teabag into the mug. The kettle reached its zenith and clicked off. Within a split second of pouring the boiling water there was a sharp crack. The seismic force split the new mug, physically moving the two halves. Like book ends they faced each other in a pool of warm brown water, the sodden teabag slumped between like a lost cause.

Tuesday 31st July. The seasons were changing. As far as the eye could see, the inferno of wavering grasses had been cut, the sorrel, the thistles, and the flowers too. Nothing was spared. Everything had been cut and lay tedded, exposed to the sun and the wind in faded yellowing windrows waiting to be baled.

The hay had been cut late into the evening and stretched on into the night. Great beams like search lights flared over the field, harvesting in long straight strips turning in a big wide sweep then back again in long straight strips, the darkness in hefty hulking shadows thrown about, the drone, deep in the ground.

The sweet grassy alpine smell, lingered in the air as her feet disturbed the grass. It was hard to believe that it was now as dry as it had been wet. For once her boots were almost completely dry and mud free. She stooped to re-tie her lace. Now the only thing to concern her about walking alone was if she misjudged the height of the stile and crashed to the ground or accidently tripped and fell down a rabbit hole like Alice.

Since the bid seven years ago there had been no let-up in the hype about the 2012 Olympics and obviously in the run-up to it, it had increased to saturation point. Newspapers were thick with facts and figures, advertisers glamourized and television followed the blazing Olympic Torch Relay around the country, honing in nightly on streets lined with people cheering and waving flags. Everyone seemed to be interested except her, that was, until she met her friend in the toothpaste aisle on Friday morning. Having not seen her for a few weeks they shared their news. Sworn to secrecy, she said that she had worked on the costumes for the opening ceremony in a week's time and that she had been invited to the rehearsal and was buzzing with enthusiasm. From then on she paid more attention, going as far as buying a paper with an 'Essential 60-page guide to the greatest show on earth,' free, leaving it splayed on the dresser to browse through the programme of events.

She had been in two minds about taking her book, but in the end had left it on the side. How she wished she had it.

Emergency engineering work was being carried out on the track and there were no trains running. The first train to leave was half an hour later than she expected and once everyone was on it, the delay continued for a further 20 minutes. People were on their phones, relaying the problem and the constant opening and closing of doors gave the impression that the train was about to depart. There was a collective sigh throughout the carriage when the train finally pulled away. Timetabled to stop at all stations, the train laboured and groaned with fraught passengers. Immersing herself in her book would have given her solace and distracted her from the irritation of wasting so much time. Her plan to walk the quiet London streets and breakfast on the corner listening to the pealing bells was abandoned. Instead, she dashed down the escalator and onto the Northern line to Leicester Square to walk the short way to Trafalgar Square. Arriving late, she quietly filed into a pew at the back of the church and drew breath. Like others coming in late, she had made it. Stepping outside into the sunshine an hour later she crossed the road to Trafalgar Square, disappointingly shrouded in various canvas arrangements, a stage and satellite stalls, tacky dance music blaring to no-one, a barrier preventing access and security asking questions. Why, when there were going to be visitors from all over the world, did the powers that be have to spoil such a fine historic vista? Plunging back into the underground, she took herself off to Hornchurch, the reason for going into London, to watch the Olympic Torch Relay. Arriving with time to spare she had lunch and sat in the brilliant sunshine watching the crowds accumulate along the road. Just after two she stood and waited on the pavement. Out of cavernous bags, hawkers ran between the crowds selling flags and medals and horns. Excitement flared as the cavalcade neared. The people clamoured and swarmed into the road hoping for a glimpse of the flame. The road teemed with police on bikes, in vans and in quiet smooth cars, their presence hoping to dispel any potential trouble. As the flame was carried high everyone cheered and she took the all-important picture, disappearing back into the station almost as soon as it had passed.

THE OLYMPICS

As her husband powered the TV controls, it was hard to say that they sat down to watch the opening ceremony, but from nine they did see most of it in between Forever Young, When Rock 'n' Roll Grew Up and The Shipping Forecast. The technical achievements were amazing. Danny Boyle painted an affectionate picture of centuries of history and culture, transforming the arena from a countryside idyll to an industrial landscape where chimneys belching smoke emerged and the Olympic rings were seen to be forged to the present day of instant communication, music and film. Each spectacular scene was peppered with little interruptions of drama and poetry, along with splashes of music and clever computer graphics, even the Queen took part, parachuting in with James Bond and Rowan Atkinson ran along the West Sands in St Andrews as depicted in Chariots of Fire, leading up the to the athletes and their entourages proudly walking into the arena, their flags held proudly high and finally lighting the cauldron. In the meantime David Beckham was whipping along the Thames in a speed boat to deliver the flame that was taken from him by Steve Redgrave who in turn passed it on to six young athletes to light the centre piece of copper petals. Flawlessly the petals closed to form the flame, starting the real pageant of skill, endurance, tears, strength, determination, desire, guts, stamina, fatigue, effort, relief, disappointment, fulfilment and hope. By the end of the evening a surge of pride, not felt for a long time spread through her.

On and off they watched the road cycling together. Her husband kept in contact with their two sons who were watching the event in Richmond Park. The media had assured that Team GB were in with a chance. Waiting and watching in the throng of people lining the route through Richmond Park were their two sons and her husband contacted them with them every few minutes updating the progress of the race. Once over Putney Bridge, she knew the route to the finishing line. Suddenly Kazakhstan and Columbia pulled away, until then there had been no mention of their threat.

She watched the synchronized diving, superb, but found it hard to watch the swimming, it was too nerve wracking, she kept getting up and leaving the room. On and off she glanced at the football, much to her husband's surprise, England were playing UAE, at times so frustrating but she found herself gasping with relief when the third goal was scored and the team were through to the next round, not that she wanted her husband to think that her exclamation construed that she had suddenly adopted any pleasure in the sport. It was so unlike the usual games on TV being without the frenetic in-your-face advertising hoardings flashing round the pitch and the team's strip disguised with so many logos to become distracting, there was more focus on the technical skill that so often becomes lost. The hoardings were plain and unpretentious in their Cadbury Milk Tray colours.

Together they watched the hockey, GB against rivals Argentina and turned over at half time to the swimming then back to the hockey then back to the swimming then back to the hockey, which GB won, then over to the nail-biting finish of the basketball, along with a jab of boxing, the clean and jerk of weightlifting and all the strength and agility that the GB artistic gymnastics team could muster to secure their bronze medal. Then they watched the fighting in Aleppo.

On Tuesday after several attempts she turned the TV on only to hold her breath at every jump of the equestrian events, then, when her husband came in they watched the women's football at Wembley, GB versus Brazil which GB won with a quick plunge to the Aquatic Centre to check the swimming and Horse Guards Parade to glance at the volleyball against Australia.

Until Surrey won, cricket from Trent Bridge took precedence over the Olympics. In between there were quick blinks of volleyball and hockey with their huddles and pep-talks, neither of which changed the result, until the football against Uruguay, won by GB, came on, then on and off channel hopping to the Aquatic Centre and the Excel Arena to watch the Italian snapping and snarling at GB's heals.

Gemma Gibbons's judo performance brought a lump to her husband's throat and they watched Peter Wilson shatter the clay pigeons into florescent pink dust over the shooting range. All day the results had been good and there was no doubt that the woman's team sprint at the Velodrome was going to be a gold medal for Victoria Pendleton and Jessica Varnish. The energetic level of noise and sporting exuberance from the crowd was deafening. But after a shattering world record lap they were cruelly disqualified. Although they followed the women's hockey, and what an excellent victory it was for GB, she and her husband never quite got over the disappointment.

Happy enough, she spent the day quietly on her own, swimming, gardening, reading and writing. Not only did she have to listen to the TV commentators but her husband came in throwing his comments and criticisms and voicing his opinions to her. It was Victoria Pendelton's day. For weeks the media had over exposed a number of athletes and imposed an unrealistic weight of expectation loaded with hope to win on the athletes. The pressure to live up to the demands sometimes fell short as did Rebecca Adlington's freestyle, left her feeling that she wanted to apologise and that winning a bronze just wasn't good enough. Like a mushrooming cloud the momentum was starting to build, the atmosphere in the Olympic Park was electric. After the swimming they watched Jessica Ennis, and heard the mad explosion from the passionate crowd as she ran in the next event. Then, on and off they watched the quiet unassuming Ethiopian woman win the 10,000mtrs in between A People's History.

Saturday was hailed as the greatest night, celebrating six gold medals. Carried on a wave of emotion Mo Farah won the 10,000 metres, Greg Rutherford won a gold medal in the long jump and Jessica Ennis throbbing with effort, ran and won the 800 metres to complete the most truly outstanding heptathlon performance, ever. The crowd went wild and of course the next day the papers devoted pages and pages to photos and reports on their success.

Quietly, Christine Ohuruogu won silver in the 400 metres, almost drowned out by the big event of the day, the 100 metres final and the cruel elimination in the heats beforehand of all except the first two over the finishing line resulting in the fastest men on the planet in the final line-up. Pushing the boundaries, Jamaicans Mr Bolt was first, Mr Blake was second and Mr Gatlin of the USA was third. In ten seconds she could barely achieve anything more than wrestle with a bin bag and she did not come remotely close to lacing one boot and she was hard pushed to thread her sewing machine or mash a tea bag. The thing that amused her while the athletes were warming-up, was the girl standing in the frame behind the strapping Mr Bolt. Her lingering eyes followed his every move as he subtly removed each layer of clothing down to his long lean beautiful black limbs. Sometimes she found herself looking at the pale gold face of her watch which except for the three that had a little window for the date, the numbers were marked with a thin gold line and the minutes between each an even thinner and shorter black line, the second hand was thinner than a hair and the minute hands sandwiched the thinnest fluorescent line, not to see the time but to see if the second hand moved five times between each number. Sometimes it seemed to be still, so still that she thought it had stopped but amazingly there was time for Mr Bolt to pull out the stops in one second and run ten meters.

They remembered being bored witless when they were young watching The Horse of the Year Show on TV, well in those days you watched everything, even the boxing, but at every jump she sensed her husband, like she, was on the settee, lifting his hooves, to clear the fence in the team show jumping. Later, on her third attempt, Holly Bleasdale cleared the pole vault bar comfortably then she made herself a little den out of barriers draped with towels to wait for the height of the bar to be increased to find only minutes later bitter disappointment, as did Dai Green in the 400 metres hurdles, for the only white man, it was a daunting task, and to finish at all let alone fourth was to be recommended. The team at Mission Control leapt with relief when after four years, Curiosity landed on Mars.

A rich seam of gold had been tapped at the Velodrome with yet more medals, for Chris Hoy and Laura Trott. It had been another great day for the athletes and the spectators. Mr and Mrs Brownlee glowed with pride at their sons' success.

Women continued to make their mark. Jade Jones won gold in taekwondo and Nicola Adams won gold in the women's flyweight boxing.

After a day of no medals team GB returned to the roaring crowds.

Being busy on Friday and Saturday her husband kept her informed with news and progress of the events as they happened running out into the garden on Sunday afternoon to tell her that Anthony Joshua had won gold in the super-heavyweight fight.

Instead of sixteen days of tedium it had been a feast of celebration, of highs and lows and blood sweat and tears. From the beginning they were gunning for Team GB and they weren't taking any prisoners. From their armchairs she and her husband grew hooves and jumped fences, they pressed their feet into pedals, dropped sails, pulled and pushed and threw and hurled themselves forward and over and ran like the wind with the competitors. From the athletes there had been an outstanding endeavour. She didn't think she could remember another time in her life when the whole country didn't seem weighted down with doom and gloom. Like a form of mass bullying, after a while it was so demoralizing. The 2012 Olympics had been uplifting, the country was buoyant, and people were genuinely interested, like having a common goal.

The Olympics prompted a swimming resurgence and the 10 o'clock 'adults' only session was packed. Inspired Olympians vied for a straight length, jostling for position, finding a gap and filling it. Some swimmers, men, thought that it was the Aquatics Centre, powering along, tumble turning at the end. Most however, were ladies, their heads gently bobbing like seals from end to end, having a chat.

For two weeks they had feasted on the unexpected instead of the predictable, knowing that the diet of tepid news and lukewarm programmes would return. The athletes' glory had been commemorated on stamps and post boxes had been sprayed gold. Local newspapers had featured their stories along with childhood photos.

The legacy, what legacy? Already, with the excitement extinguished, the petals of the cauldron still warm and the flame 'bound for the Rio Grande' there were murmurs of lucrative marketing deals, raised profiles, estimations of the money that could be earned from and for athletes at the top of their game. To her it was the seedy side, someone making mega bucks out of a split second, or good luck or someone else's bad luck. Why couldn't they be left alone 'to be a hero, just for the day'? Sport in schools was thrown about, two hours a day suggested. When, in the timetable was there time to do two hours a day, only at the expense of other subjects. Probably more than half the children anyway did not like participation in any sport, it was endured. When she was out and about there were very few children playing out, playing football or cricket, facilities for other sports were few and far between and while many went to the various clubs, it was not necessarily because they enjoyed it, more because parents bribed or coerced or made them go. At school some would avoid PE like the plague, producing a forged sick note from their top pocket or feigning lost kit or simply hide in the toilets for the double lesson.

For her the legacy would be the memories and the unbelievable spectacle. Too quickly the hype subsided and by Tuesday the Olympics were barely mentioned. The increase in rail fares, the economy, how local election funding would change and the conflict in Syria were on the agenda. Less than a week later the Olympics did not make the national news. Melancholia resumed.

5

There seemed a hundred jobs that needed attention before fixing the Tiverton Grey kitchen units that were leaning in the hall, in place. The kitchen roof needed insulating and although nothing to do with the kitchen the guttering needed replacing at the back of the house. Duly delivered were 14 rolls of insulation and two 4 metre lengths of guttering. The new kitchen was accumulating in the hall. The old kitchen was accumulating in the dining room. Cupboards were emptied and stored in plastic storage boxes on and under the table. Each time she needed an ingredient she had to go into the dining room to retrieve it.

Where possible she progressed as far as she could without help or an extra pair of hands for lifting. Once again, out came the wallpaper stripper. Being hung on reasonably new walls compared to those in the rest of the house, the lovely William Morris wallpaper came away in good sized pieces. Like a Chinese Laundry the humidity was high. In the steam bath of old glue and plaster her hair got bigger and her glasses fogged. The back door was flung open. With the cupboards emptied she started to dismantle the units, unhinging the oak doors and unscrewing the fittings she lifted out the shelves, installed with her son's help when he was just a teenager, remembering using a drill that kept sparking and hoping that it would not blow a fuse. Now six gaping mouths stared blankly back at her, where for years cereals and suet and jam and spices and children had hidden, she wanted to close the imaginary doors.

On her way to B&Q she saw Lady Godiva. She had seen her the previous evening on TV being presented with her size

72 leather boots made by Horace Batten, a Wellingborough boot maker in Northampton. Lady Godiva was a 10 metre high puppet and along with her giant metal horse she was powered by a team of a 100 cyclists and an army of puppeteers on her way to the Olympic Games. She was not always fond of these garish, grandiose oddities, finding them strangely grotesque in a frightening sort of way, like canal art and fun fairs, slowly daring herself to look. Godiva Awakes however was not freakish or scary, her face was fairly Anglo Saxon, her short hair golden and her limbs modestly covered with demure fabrics. The only odd thing at all was that she had randomly seen her on her way to buying two tubs of masonry paint.

Thursday 2nd August. How could it be August already? She walked where streams had trickled and ponds had formed. At last they had dried up and she walked in ordinary shoes. The wind ruffled the surface of the river and blew airily drying the soft hay windrows of tangled grass. Apart from the charcoaled remains across the path and a shred of charred sepia coloured paper, Exercise 5B was the only evidence left of the fire. It was funny how the sky was full of cloud, yet it remained sunny.

Monday 6th August. As she slipped between the metal gate and the stone wall she could see a crowd of people waiting around on the path, ramblers. Seeing them, made her feel hot and hardly taking her eyes from the grass she overtook them all as quickly as possible, striding through the grass beside the path. With Sunday's torrential rain the now brown sodden hay lay still, matted and smelly. How she wanted to remove her jumper, but it would take too long, requiring her to stop and put her umbrella down and she had visions of getting her hair and her hair slides and glasses all tangled up, deciding that there wasn't time. Also, it was a recipe for losing an earring. Daring to glance behind, they were there, hot on her tail, if she stopped now they would catch her up and she would feel silly, like an Audi overtaking only to wait at the red light like everybody else. So with continued feverish urgency she kept up the furious pace, breathing in the dank heady smells of the undergrowth of the narrow track. Here and there hooves, bike tyres and footprints indented the cloying slippery mud. It was recycling day and she could hear the sound of shattering glass as the recycling boxes were dropped to the path round the houses on the other side of the encroaching hedge, followed by the drone of the lorries as they pulled away from the kerb. Maybe the rambler's group had had prior warning, the cows were at the far end of the field and the farm dogs were in their kennel. Only when she reached the field deep in rough dried rape seed on the other side of the farm did she remove her jumper. Her keys and voice recorder she tucked low in her jeans pockets, the stretch denim gripping them snugly and her umbrella went down her sleeve as she thankfully at last peeled off her jumper. The ramblers were nowhere in sight and she took that to mean that they had gone another way and not done the circular walk after all or she had outpaced them. Either way she could slow down; through the gap where there had once been a gate to the next farm and along the narrow road to the next gate. The ripening fields went on and on, behind the trees to the curved horizon where they touched the changeable sky. Even though she didn't see him she knew the laugh to be that of the green woodpecker. Overhead, the lime leaves pattered. Unable to dislodge the handle on the unyielding gate she climbed over it as others had done, she could see where a muddied boot had split the wood, and into her favourite field, the perfect golden piecrust field with a wide, recently mown grassy path around the edge. She knew that sound, too, that of a curlew. On her way round the great swathe of wheat she disturbed butterflies and dragonflies. Ahead, seven wind turbines sliced through the air. Above her the willows heaved about and in the silence where she walked she could hear the relentless rasping breath of the motorway. The path followed into the sleepy hamlet of Lathbury. There was a crating sound. She liked to think it was a corn crake, but probably more likely to be a pheasant, hoarse and out of tune. Crossing the last two meadows she found herself on the main road. Until she walked the few hundred yards into town, she felt conspicuous, the traffic was noisy and the hedge was littered with disposable cups and sandwich boxes and chocolate bar wrappers, casually thrown from car windows.

The gas was capped and until the oven was removed her eye kept returning to the neon numbers of the digital clock, which, unless there had been a power cut, had reliably shown the time for more than thirty years.

From the moment the gas was capped, meals, as she knew them, ceased. The magically unfolding two burner camping stove was manufactured in Britain by Pandora and bought in their pioneering days when she and her then boyfriend drove to Spain in the late sixties. The field kitchen was set up outside the back door, the camping stove placed on the Workmate and the gas bottle on an upturned bucket. Cooking outside became innovative. Boiling and frying were the new cooking methods, making burgers, kidneys, potato salad, poaching fish, spicy chicken, stir fries, liver and onions, kippers, curry, spaghetti bolognaise, chilli. Keeping food hot was a problem especially when cooking for a crowd. The dining room resembled a crammed furniture store, there was a narrow twelve inch galley between the six foot dresser and the two tables and it was in this gap that she prepared food on the wooden chopping board, made toast and boiled the kettle. In a brand new bucket she drew water from the tap in the outside toilet. Her 20 square metres of kitchen had been reduced to one, doing anything other than the bare necessities in the confines of the limited space was exacting. If she had a cat, there was not enough room to swing it. After three weeks without mains gas she succumbed to a hearty lunch of fish and chips, courtesy of The Golden Fry, if she were honest it was more because of the gale force wind and intermittent rain. For her fish and chips was the ultimate comfort food, steeped in fat, filling and vaguely nutritious having all the qualities to guarantee pleasurable satisfaction. Through the window she could see two filets bubbling with batter in the hot lock. Coming back moments later from posting a letter they had gone in as an old man was leaving the shop with his dinner tucked under his arm, leaving her to stand and wait at the side for more fish to be fried. While she waited a boy came along and threw down his bike all over the pavement, marched in wanting chips immediately, then a woman like her wanted fish and chips and she, too, had to wait. The owner, a beady black-eyed Cypriot was in complete charge of the frying, he slapped the glistening fish to and fro in the tub of batter and immersed the pieces of fish expertly into the fryer. The chips were already ready and the next bucket of them stood on the floor. To his side, a stunning girl, dark hair tied back. A silver dolphin hung at her throat. Waiting, she had the time to envy her, the way her bare arms effortlessly moved like taut rubber bands and her smooth flawless skin. She watched Tina going about her job, which in between serving meant wiping the sides and standing attentively beautiful. Out of her eye Tina caught sight of a long single loose black hair moulded to her tee shirt. It had to be removed. Looking completely unfazed she nonchalantly pinched the offensive hair and casually let it drift to the floor. The fish was ready. Deftly Tina made a move, onto the white sheets of paper placed just so on the stainless steel counter she placed a scoop of chips in the greaseproof paper bag followed by another scoop followed by the fish that perched on top. "Salt and vinegar?" She asked and she nodded in reply mesmerised with the speed of the dextrous wrapping as she tucked it in a paper bag. The procedure was repeated. "That's £10 please."

She imagined that the walls dividing each cupboard would, with one blow, be reduced to a pile of rubble. It was not to be. Her husband had built them to last, keyed into the main structure of the house they were stubborn, kiln fired brick, nothing short of solidified magma with the density of a meteorite, requiring a blow of determination and the strength of an ox. Very few remained whole. The air was thick with brick dust, the floor crunched with grit. Slowly she cleared the piles of brick to the wheelbarrow which her husband insisted on wheeling to the end of the garden for the foundations of the shed. The oven and the hob were removed from their housing, everything that could be removed, doors, shelves, linings, was, lightening the weight, allowing her to transport it to the dump more easily. It took two trips. By her second trip the metal container had been emptied and she saw her oven perched on top of the blue scrap metal lorry leaving the yard. On reaching the sink, they called it a day, sweeping and vacuuming and wiping the brick dust until it was habitable. The next day the blue sack barrow wheeled the fridge/freezer into position in the dining room, the last of the walls were demolished and the cushion flooring was lifted, leaving a desperate disintegrating rubberized residue. The smell of the old floor greeted her when she opened the door that she tried her best to keep shut in order to avoid the pungent rubbery smell and pervasive dust dispersing through the entire house. Only the sink, finely balanced, remained. Days later she still went to where the fridge had been to return the milk. Using a bolster and a hammer she chipped away at the tiles, filling two big tubs, then between the showers she loaded the car with them and the folded-up flooring piled outside and went to the dump. The wiring was started and boxes drawn on the wall to indicate sockets and cabling. Laid out on a piece of worktop on the kitchen table were all the surgical instruments required for the operation. The kitchen looked like a war zone, pockmarked and acned with rawlplug holes, gouged where the wiring had been ripped out, pipes hanging by a thread. It was sorrowful. In less than a week it was no more than an empty shell, anorexic, bare bones, no skirting, no coving, the hidden corners revealed, crude where the ceiling met the walls and where the walls met the floor. Her son sat at the end of the dust-covered kitchen table browsing through the Screw Fix Catalogue, selecting various components required for the wiring, composing a list as he went on a side of A4 paper. With 1050 pages in the Screw Fix book there was always something to catch your attention, something that you didn't realise you needed and couldn't live without until you saw it in print. Her husband was addicted and seeing the list reaching down the page, added another order number. She would go first thing. It was such a busy shop, even at eight in the morning. While she waited for her order to be processed she looked around. It was the shoes that caught her attention, a man was leaning in over the counter wearing pale grey jersey pyjamas and tan leather shoes, and then Greg from school appeared distracting her thoughts. Exchanging hellos across the shop he joined her in the queue. It was A level results day and he had got an A in Resistant Materials. He was chuffed to bits. Regardless of what the day threw at him, she knew that he would have a smile pasted to his face all day. As she paid, the assistant quickly asked if she would like to make a rash purchase of a tape measure from the point of sale tub by the till. How many tape measures did she need? The fan was removed and like the cupboard tops was thick with grease, having the sticky feel of a fly paper. The black hole in the wall from whence it came was brushed and cleaned. Through the vents she saw the sky and the Virginia creeper shivering against the wall in the restless wind. She could no longer keep pace with the grey dust that coated everything, she could write her name in it.

Wednesday 8th August. For the first time in over a year they sat on the sun-drenched pavement outside the Dolphin. It was the ideal spot to watch the world go by and enjoy a drink at the same time. While her husband popped into the bank she located a table and sat facing the sun, whiling her time watching the traffic and people toing and froing until he reappeared to check again what she wanted to drink. Standing up to leave, a couple of drinks later, she said "Shall we go and look at the river?" At a leisurely pace they set out across the field and over the stile to walk beside the water. Under the round yellow sun they walked on their stunted disfigured shadows. For her husband it was nostalgic, remembering how it used to be, remembering what fish he had caught and where he had caught them from. All the way to the wire fence he gave a running commentary. It was a perfect afternoon and the river was dark and glassy calm. The windrows had still not been baled. Walking back, they caught sight of a barn owl. It was a daring flight, driven out into the open in broad daylight, noiselessly sweeping the field in a desperate search for food. There was no mistaking the creamy buff plumage and the feathery ruff. Gaining height he gracefully veered away, banking round the hedge to land in the pitiful ivy clad limbs of the ash tree, where the gardens backed onto the field.

Friday 10th August. Feeling ambitious, two days later, he said to her "Shall we walk to the canal?" They walked via The Railway Walk, virtually a straight path of Tarmac which until 1967 when Dr Beeching's slash and burn policies were introduced, it had been the railway line. Other than being a direct route and especially suitable for bikes it was fairly nondescript. The good thing, albeit an ambitious six miles for her husband, was that they were taking a walk. Reaching the platform in Great Linford they turned off for the canal. Walking one behind the other they walked the narrow worn out tow-path, stopping every now and then for her husband to imagine what lay beneath the tempting yellow border of water lilies on the far bank. It was warm and summery. Her husband had started well, but once away from the draw of the canal he lost interest, anxious that his lead heavy legs would get him home.

Thursday 16th August. It was her sister's birthday. Shutting the doors on the billowing dust, she went out. It was dull and warm and windy. Getting the road bit out of the way, she found herself through the kissing gate following the winding trodden grassy path across the first meadow. The ewes ambled about too intent on nibbling to notice her. In the distance, against the backcloth of blustering cloud, she could see her special field, lighter than ever. Nearer, she imagined the farmer going around surveying the crop, checking the yield that was already suffering from the erratic weather, taking an ear of wheat and rubbing it between his finger and thumb, instinctively knowing if it was ready to harvest, casually dropping it for the chaff to lightly disperse and the grain to be gathered by a lucky field mouse out gathering provisions. The pale gold sweep rustled gently in the wind, above however, the willows were riotous, writhing and twisting, their silvery green leaves flipped over, their chafing branches squeaking like rusting hinges. Elaborately entwined elderberries and clusters of haws were ripening in the hedgerows. Already fields were ploughed and being ploughed, she could see a plough lifting and turning the soil, incorporating the stubble. Groaning up and down, up and down, gulls in toe, gleaning something to eat. Looking at her watch, exactly an hour later and approximately half way round the circular walk, she exclaimed hooray to the big wide sky. The awful scratchy rape seed field had been cut. Everything had been cut, the track blended with the fields either side, looking like one enormous field. Glad of the wind touching her skin she turned left following the spent and dying seam of redleg towards the farm. Farms seemed to operate like road works, nothing ever seemed to be happening then suddenly the harvest was in and the next crop was sown. Not seeing the cows at all as she walked down towards the river and the first cattle grid was good, the uncertainty of them being there and having to back-track or brave the murky light below the motorway had been irking her, but they were settled further away in the next field. In the narrow airless weed-choked track, the blackberry briars and the black and mouldering stems of spindly nettles reached out for light across the path. In places it was a bit of a dumping ground for garden waste, just thrown over the garden fences, out of sight, out of mind. Bury Field was green. Overnight the windrows had been baled and taken away. Like strands of hair the remnants of the hay lay around amongst the soft springy grass.

It was the 23rd of August. It was a significant date, one that she remembered writing on the whiteboard in March. It was the morning of the GCSE results and just a little bit of her was curious to know how well her students had done in their exams. It had been such a mixed ability group anything was possible. She hoped that they had pulled out the stops. Breathing a sigh of relief she no longer worried about finding the neatly stapled wodge of paperwork in her pigeon hole on the first day of term detailing lists and data in coloured graphs and charts highlighting disappointments, with the words value added and residual to discuss later in the day. Until she stopped working, she hadn't realized how much the demands of her job sapped her energy, grinding down and consuming every living cell. She pictured the agenda word processed in July starting with the all-important whole staff meeting in the theatre, the whole compliment of staff sitting in the tiered seating on tip up seats, wistfully talking about the holidays they had taken. Then senior staff would present the exam results, the facts and figures, death by power-point. By 9.15am – "Now where did I go on holiday?"

The plastering was the next instalment. Unlike the floor, it wasn't something she could choose and knew little other than it usually involved a bath and lightning speed and that plasterers were known for how much mess they created. Tanned and fresh from Turkey the plasterer arrived at 8.20am. Lean and brown he stood around her shell of a kitchen and made notes, quoting her a price. She draped the cupboards with dust sheets and the floor with an old shower curtain and dust sheets anchored down with masking tape to protect against the inevitable spills and splashes. Friday morning was still and cool. Ribbons of condensation streamed down the windows. A dark wetness exuded from the newly plastered walls. It had the smell of a cave and took days to dry. Shaking the dust sheets outside she vacuumed the floor and with her husband's help lifted the table back into the kitchen. They ate in their newly plastered kitchen. She laid a clean cloth on the table. Her husband faced the window and she sat opposite him. It felt like they were lovers, their voices carried in the empty echoing room, the food was incidental.

Monday 27th August. It was August Bank Holiday Monday. Spared the heavy rain that fell in most parts of the country, it was dull and there was an autumnal feel in the air. Feeling dislocated and unable to do anything much in the house she went out under the pretence of needing milk. As the horses were not in their field by the river she crossed the stile. On the back of the strengthening wind, angry clouds billowed through, the brooding sky darkened and the air grew cool. Rain threatened. In places where the wind disturbed, the ruffled surface of the river was dabbed with grey light. Swallows dipped and swooped. Dandelions emerged again. Walking into town to get the milk she stopped to browse at a vase that she simply didn't need. Arriving home, the plasterer had folded his step ladder and was making for the door. Shaking the dust sheets in the garden, she folded them and vacuumed the floor.

It was good to meet up with her patient friend and proof-reader of her books. Her generosity could not be measured, providing advice, technical support and guidance, a scaffolding, to enable her to step onto the precarious wrung of the publishing ladder. To her it seemed an imposition to expect anyone to take on the epic task of proof reading, resulting in the last manuscript being sent to the publishers without her dedicated scrutiny and she had to admit that the criticisms were justified.

Ordering two large coffees, they took up their familiar seat almost out of sight inside the door. Two years had passed since meeting as they once did to discuss the use of hyphens and position of speech marks and exchange drafts secreted in carrier bags for her inspection. They settled and their coffees arrived. They talked, absorbed in their great clutch of children that between them they shared, concluding that children were for life and that even into their thirties, the fragility of their lives – the hoping and longing that never comes, disappointments, the frustrations of relationships and work playing their part in equal measure – still sent them hurtling home to the familiar bolt-hole, the safe sanctuary of home until the eye of the storm within themselves had passed. Her friend was a grandmother and her daughters juggled motherhood with their careers. It was never straight forward for girls. For sons and daughters expectations were impossibly high. Some forever lived in shadows, their dreams unfulfilled. Only the other day while collecting her son from the station she caught sight of him. He was agitated. He knew she was there, waiting, parked in the mayhem and although he wanted to sink into the safety of the seat beside her, he just couldn't bring himself to walk the few steps to the car. He needed a moment knowing that what he was going to say would spoil her reverie. Also he would have felt some degree of shame, his mother seeing him unable to cope without the crutch of a nicotine fix. Having given him the clearest, purest, healthiest lungs it vexed her terribly to see them damaged by the wretched addiction. She didn't say anything. She didn't need to. He knew what she thought. It was Friday and commuters spewed from the London train, storming out into the warm evening sunshine. The first off-peak train had been rammed and uncomfortably hot and the air conditioning added a deafening scream of air between the stations, sticky exhaustion subdued the passengers, people stood and sat on the floor by the doors putting up with anything just to get home.

Already he had been in a smoking-free zone for an hour and she pictured him busy in his bag, gathering the all-too-familiar components together and with meticulous precision pull a rolling paper from its little box, feed a filter tip from its fine tube of cellophane then lining it up with the edge of the paper, tease a pinch of tobacco along the remaining length of paper, then discretely taking his tongue along the edge of glue, rolled it expertly into thin tight tube. Returning all the paraphernalia to his bag he held the faultlessly crafted cigarette by the tip, ready. Urgently fumbling to light it as soon as he stepped from the station he took a deep lungful of pollution. He exhaled slowly. With a pang of regret she turned her head away. He had a way of holding a cigarette, encompassed and concealed within his fingers. Throwing the butt to the ground, he pressed the life from it. His body language said it all and before he hugged and smiled his easy smile and said a warm hello the haemorrhage started, ripping into his monologue, barely stopping to draw breath he spat venom about the absurd wealth of some people. Immediately she felt weighted down with his anger and tension. The stress of his working week filled her car. Excited to see her children, lovingly doing their rooms, shopping for and cooking their favourite meals, she went to great lengths, but his lavish outpouring unexpectedly drained her. By Sunday evening, however, with her unconditional love for him, her patience and devotion for his wellbeing, she had more or less restored his confidence and rescued him from himself. Cautiously peering into the future they mulled over the merits of retirement, airing their aspirations and what there was yet to be done, questioning pensions and the cost of living and how frugal and creative they could be when push came to shove, resurrecting skills and passions that the demands of the working day had prohibited. Outside the rain persisted, the pavements shone.

PARALYMPICS

The athletes had all the hallmarks of the Olympians, the drive, the courage, the gumption but with additional mountainous frustrations of being disabled and the prejudice and intolerance that accompanies anyone who does not conform to the norm. The athletes were inspirational. Technology had revolutionized the basic flesh coloured plastic prosthesis, legs were like angle-poise lamps or windscreen wipers striding out like pylons. Alas she didn't follow the event in the same way as the Olympics, but nevertheless she was still keen to follow the medal tally and she watched and listened when she could. The athletes were not interested in the patronizing pity that crept into reporting, it was a genuine sporting spectacle and the athletes were motivated in the same way as those in the previous games, nonetheless the media and the newspapers kept up the fervour playing on the emotional narrative. It was cynical but she didn't think that the 'new' attitude towards disabled people would last long. While she and her son took to the flight of steps outside Euston, a man, sat cluttering the access in a wheelchair, urinated. It poured through his seat onto the pavement. There were people everywhere, stepping round him and over the water trickling into the gutter. He looked around helplessly. Like everyone else, she and her son avoided him.

Thursday 30th August. Basically she went out because her husband was badgering for a tube of Super Glue and until she went he wouldn't settle. She could see that this could happen frequently as the dourweather encroached. Very slightly annoyed, like the clouds scudding through, her thoughts kept on coming. Women, she thought, were loyal to their husbands and guilty of not saying what they really wanted to say about how they would fare with their husbands at home all day, not blaming them but giving other reasons like how they would fill their time. Behind her, distracting her from her negative thoughts, two white Scotties pulling like beads on a lead, anxious to be running about. All the way she stomped along in the biting north easterly wind. Of course, to please, she didn't forget the glue.

6

Monday saw the start of the new floor. Up early, she vacuumed for the last time. Little nuggets of brick and blisters of plaster rattled their way to the new bag swelling beneath Mr Henry's smiling plastic face, and other things like a piece of missing jig-saw puzzle, last seen, mmm don't know when, and a red crayon, the set incomplete, they too jangled their way up the pipe and along the curling hose to join the hard-core. As arranged, workers Dave and Gary arrived at 8am. Firstly the floor was washed with an evil looking aquamarine sealant and left to dry. Then it was flooded with concrete coloured syrupy latex. It was chocolaty smooth and in its wet glassy surface the window shone back. Along with their son, she and her husband filed into in the dining room congested with the old kitchen to admire the latex, like an installation to be marvelled at in the Tate Modern. The process of drying could be a piece of artwork in itself, captured on a twelve hour video, set up on a loop, a single bench opposite the screen for people with nothing better to do than watch paint dry. Well, it could be anything you wanted it to be. For her it was where the gentle wash of the tide receding until it was no more, silently seeping, bleeding away, leaving pale hard flat sand, the last rivulets withdrawn to leave a sweep of gravelly deposit. It was as flat as flat could be.

There seemed nothing she could do, so she sat instead on the swivel chair, absently swivelling until she had a thought, idly making shapes with a large rubber band on her lap and writing random words in her notebook while at the same time talking to her son as he filled his cavernous ruck-sack with holiday necessities, taking great delight in showing her and demonstrating his pocket rocket cooker and washing-up bowl that neatly folded into a little pouch the size of a tin of floor polish.

The next day, futuristic red laser beams surveyed, zipping pencil-thin right-angled lightening lines of light across the kitchen floor. Retractable tape measures were extended and contracted to clatter back into their casings. Tools jingled on the hard flat surface. From her swivel chair upstairs she could hear the sweep of a trowel. Now and then there was a gentle tapping and when there was something to say she heard their voices or laughing, sometimes they absently whistled or sang along with a song playing on their little radio sitting on the windowsill. The hollow echoing kitchen made for good acoustics. Slipping downstairs for a drink she peered in to see the progress, the adhesive was carefully combed into place and guided by the zip of red light each tile was expertly positioned with meticulous accuracy. The floor was taking shape.

With no son to distract her, he had gone with his girlfriend on holiday to Norway she sat at the computer catching up with her writing. All the time she thought about words – wrapping words around each other, making sentences and paragraphs – sparking thoughts and triggering memories, never knowing where it would lead suddenly there would be a page or a chapter. She had a great desire to write things down as they actually happened or as near as possible, in a language that was accessible to all. Not like a reporter, larger than life, exaggerated for effect, but to make it real and true, how it really was. She wanted to record the mundane, everyday things that could be overlooked and barely worth mentioning but felt that it was those threads that held everything together. In her writing she wanted to transport her reader, for them to hear the wash of the tide in the trees, to taste the faint drift of salt in the spume, to see the vapour trail dissolve into a dinosaur's vertebrae, to breath the clean smell of washing brought in from the line, she wanted the reader to be with her, to be fed and nourished by her words, not so much to gain from her experiences but to realize that they too could look at life differently, to see that what they might dismiss as being incidental or boring was far from being so.

Averse to long-winded sentences and superfluous words filling the page, she would rephrase or delete altogether. Prudent as always, she was careful with words. Having all the time in the world allowed her senses to dwell and indulge. Alert to subtle changes of light or atmosphere or mood-invoked memories she was able to linger, adding detailed depth to her words. She could see with her eyes shut, coming closer and closer, soul-searching. It was maddening, especially during the night, if she thought of a good word then instantly forgot it. Often quite simple words eluded her. Over and over again she would try and retrieve them, try to exhume them from her memory, picturing herself and looking inside her head to see what she was thinking about at the time. Imagining she could remember the first letter, she would patiently work through the dictionary for words beginning with 're' or 'ex'. In the process she was usually taken up with other words and the need to find what she was originally looking for, lessened. From time to time when flicking through the dictionary the same word would jump from the page. Very occasionally, the word, thought of in the night and forgotten unexpectedly, came flooding back into her mind during the day. At times she found herself rummaging through her bag for a pen and something, anything to write on, stopping on her way into town half way up Silver Street to write down her thoughts. Now and then erratic, clumsy words were scrawled on folded paper on the bedside table. It was enough to get the gist, better than beating herself up all day trying to recall. Keeping track of the endless pieces of paper recessed away in drawers and pockets and squirrelled under cushions was not very organised and although not always possible she tried to keep her notes in her notebook. Sometimes it was random incidents and comments she had difficulty in recalling even though they happened or were said only moments earlier. God it was frustrating. In her book she wrote in the smallest handwriting, often two or three lines to the feint and was guilty of writing her thoughts down one page then up the next and against the grain. Anything that came into her mind but belonged elsewhere was bracketed. Just to hold the little book of thoughts open on her lap soothed her, as if she was stroking a purring cat. Like a comfort blanket it went everywhere, and she wrote anywhere at any time. With continual use, her notebook thickened. A braid of elastic kept her secrets tight. As with many of the arts there had to be an element of seclusion and secrecy, not something to be shown or discussed with all and sundry. Small handwriting gave her that privacy, even in the full view of the public gaze she could get her thoughts down. She could read anything from a distance, even upside down, even shredded. She didn't think that a piece of work should be in the public domain before being assembled, collated, rehearsed or painted, until the artist or the author or the poet or the dancer or the musician was ready. She wrote things down that were hard to say out loud. She wrote things down that she had never said. She would be mortified seeing her notebook or screen left open when unexpectedly distracted to jump up and see to something, her words uncovered, words that in some cases she had held on to for years.

Afraid of her words being seen, she usually covered the notebook with another book, or a magazine, or put it out of sight, tucked it down the side of the chair, or slipped it into a drawer or a bag, or scrolled to a blank page. However hidden she was always able see the words condensed on the page.

Although the first draft was hand-written, subsequent attempts were word processed, liking the ease with which she could change or delete words or mistakes by letting the cursor run backwards across the page, letters, words and sentences simply vanishing. Larger amounts of text could be highlighted and dismissed or magically moved around. Once the bones of a book were in place she went over it again and again, editing, reframing the sentences, getting it how she wanted it to be.

Re-writing by hand would be so laborious and time consuming that she would never have embarked on her literary journey.

Sometimes, when her husband was missing her he came to see her in Joe's room where the computer stored her ideas and stood behind her in full view of the screen. Absently she would scroll down to a blank page or go to 'Find and Replace' bringing up a box on top of her writing to avoid it being read. She felt fairly confident that not even out of curiosity would he deliberately read what she had written, no more than he would open up a file or pry into her notebooks, and if she asked him to read what she had written, he usually declined.

By early afternoon she tripped off downstairs again to forage in the fridge. Already on a plate were two spears of pineapple and to that she added a slice of ham. Returning upstairs, it took all of two minutes to eat, loafing like a student on the bed. Her son called to collect his fishing tackle. They stood in the garage talking. Dave came in. Seeing it hanging on the nail he asked. "Do you mind if I borrow that saw for a minute, darling?" Instantly her son's face furled with resentment. Initially taken aback by the man's familiarity, who was this random man dissing his mother, referring to her as 'darling'? He had no right. But that was how many men were, filling the silence with their voices. Being part of the 'construction fraternity' it was to be expected like mediocre workmanship had become the norm, however her floor was anything but, the quality of precision and exactness surpassed her expectation. The grouting sharpened the appearance further and on the third day her 'stone' coloured porcelain floor was complete.

She sat in the dining room amongst the organised chaos, reading. The settee was surprisingly free of clutter, the nearby chair acted as a table for her coffee. Her son was back from Norway and his father was doing the airport run. Arriving home at around eleven there was a sudden need to feed her hungry son. Something on toast was all she could offer and he sat on the carpet, leaning against the wall opposite her telling her all about his holiday, the eagles, the wilderness, the great outdoors, kayaking, ice-caving and walking on a glacier with crampons and an ice-axe like a great adventurer. Her husband was half listening to them from the sitting room, then came to join them, perching on the side of the settee. They talked way passed bed time.

The three friends boarded the bus for Oxford. Like escaping steam the early cloud soon dissolved and it was gloriously warm. Sauntering along the High Street they made their way towards the river, straggling at times when something in a shop window caught one or another's attention, or becoming separated by a party of sight-seers, or stopping together to huddle round a little rack of end of season shoes, or for a coffee along the way. The boats jostled and bobbed beneath the Magdalen Bridge. It was her wild desire to go boating but one of her friends, having had a bad experience, was fearful of the water and the idea was abandoned; and they declined the botanical gardens because of the excessive admission charge and so slowly made their way back to perhaps take an open top bus but dawdled, absorbed in conversation and found themselves instead thinking about lunch. Sitting at a window table they ordered from the set-menu plus wine and water and bread and oil, all that was needed really. They talked, leaning in over the table, pouring wine and water and sipping with lowered voices, their heads turning to each other, or sat back speaking freely, absently taking in the view. "And that sweet city with her dreaming spires". It took all afternoon. There was no time for doing anything else. Puffing out hot air the bus home idled in bay 11.

"The train is made up of eight carriages."
That is what comes over on the Tannoy. The doors were open on the first carriage but instead of boarding she walked further down the platform, passed first class then turned round and back to the open doors to where a handful of people sat scattered, warming themselves like lizards in the shafts of sunlight that fell across the carriage. Usually she preferred to sit on the left, facing the direction that the train was going, with a window and without any obstruction to the view. Being early there was plenty of choice and she was within a whisker

of trying several seats before finally deciding. Unclipping the pull-down table for her coffee she slid into a shady seat on the right. After the incident of the plastic lid popping off and coming dangerously close to spilling into a passenger's posh carrier bag one evening she avoided the impulsive coffee. A take-away-coffee had, like the mobile phone, almost become an accessory. An international coffee shop chain had opened in her high street. In her opinion they hadn't done their research very thoroughly and she couldn't see it lasting. It thrived, how wrong could she be? A warning bleeped insistently and the doors closed.

A patchwork of yellow stubble and brown ploughed fields carpeted the undulating view stretching out before her to the beech woods of the Chilterns, a late summer view. It was perfectly still. Not a blade of grass stirred. The black snaking slip of canal temporarily stilled. Ahead a colourful hot air balloon hung motionless in the clear blue sky. Creamy frothing garlands of traveller's joy clambered wildly over the embankments. Effortlessly gliding through the stations, the train arrived in Euston. On the Jubilee line her eyes kept glancing at the slip of a girl opposite. In her hands she clutched at a spent sunflower head, working round it like a squirrel with an acorn, gnawing at the seeds. On reaching her stop she discarded it behind her, got up and left.

She was on her way to meet her son at Canary Wharf. The sun slashed between the silver buildings of steel and glass, casting coolness and darkness and slices of warmth. Standing by the Boris bikes the shadows crept away and she waited in the sun. Vapour trails criss-crossed the sky and planes circled in the gaps between the buildings, waiting to land at Heathrow. The whole area was thronging with people on their way to the various venues of the Paralympics. Appearing, her son waved and she waved back. They hugged and kissed. Rooted to the spot, they agreed that it wasn't complicated. Together they walked along the Westferry Road to Hubbub, a café-bar, for breakfast and to admire her son's artwork. She wrote a review. "People always say they will write a review and never do. I came to Hubbub yesterday and enjoyed an excellent breakfast.

To be honest I could have sat there the entire day. The windows were flung open, the sun streamed in and the soft murmuring was mildly intoxicating. I fell in love with the pictures on the wall." Catching the bus to Aldgate they checked out Giuseppe Penome's Sazio di Luce, *Space of Light*, a bronze cast of a tree with a radiant gold-leaf interior, the finest drawings on used disposable cups, an almost grotesque window seat and a special L. S. Lowry canvas of *The Procession Passing the Queen Victoria Memorial* at The Whitechapel Gallery. The day had been one of the hottest, but ended with a thin pale grey sky. Back at the station she watched her son disappear into the underground then turned her eyes to the departure

It took three days to paint the ceiling, up and down the ladder, on and off the chair. Each day she put on her 'painting clothes' and started early. She set the radio on the sill and re-laid the dust sheets. Advised by the plasterer she sealed the walls and the ceiling with watered down paint. It was the messiest of jobs, the watery wash dripped and ran down the handle of the brush and the finished effect was nothing to be proud of. The tin said 'Pure Brilliant White' and it was and very difficult to see where she had already painted. Only if she looked at a certain angle was the ceiling very slightly darker. Cautiously she dipped the narrow brush and made her way round the tricky part then licked with a wider brush across the ceiling, stretching and reaching as far as the paint would spread then dipping the brush again. She started well, enthusiastically, but it was painstaking and it could not be left for another day. On the third day she painted all the coving first, unlike the previous day, and did not need to balance the smaller brush across the tin with the fear of it falling in. Loading the brush she applied the paint and when her right arm got to aching point she transferred the brush to her left hand, not stopping until finished. It was impossible to see where she had painted so she relied on little discrepancies or a join in the coving or a spider trying its luck as a guide. Tenderly her husband removed her glasses and proceeded to clean the paint speckles from them, rubbing the lenses in mesmerising circles with the corner of his handkerchief. She thought about the bacteria.

She assumed that her son had just called in for a cup of tea but he was happy enough to start assembling the Tiverton Grey units. For almost the entire day she was the joiner's mate, unpacking boxes, decanting screws, passing tools, holding and lifting and making cups of tea. He started with the set of drawers and followed the plan to the letter. She could see exactly why some people ended up losing their cool with flat-pack furniture. Unexpectedly at four o'clock she had to go to Euston to deliver her son's passport and on her return three hours later the oven was in situ and he had turned the corner. It was looking good. Returning the next afternoon he finished them and although two cupboards sat like beached whales waiting for her husband to complete the plumbing, the hall was finally free of the new kitchen. Like the toilet seat band reassured customers that the toilet had been sanitised in hotels so the folded pieces of paper stapled over each oven handle assured that the quality control inspection had been completed.

The nearest builder's merchants was B & Q and she quickly became familiar with the layout of the store especially 15mm copper pipe fittings and 40mm plastic pipe fittings, elbows and tees. She went armed with little lists of measurements and drawings of the parts required or even an example torn from the Screw Fix catalogue.

Only the self-service tills were open. Carefully, so that the things didn't roll off, she placed several unwieldy lengths of foam lagging, the light pendants and the jab saw on the inadequate counter at the right-hand side of the till and pressed the screen. The fear of getting it wrong at such a till was always there, but she proceeded cautiously, too cautiously for the till. While the light fittings went through safely to the left-hand side of the till, there was barely time to pick up a strip of lagging, locate the bar-code, scan it and put it down again before a voice like a Dalek insisted. "Please scan the bar-code. Please scan the bar-code." When she scanned the jab-saw, the red light flashed for the assistant's attention and the voice cut in again implying that her age needed to be verified. She stood feeling helpless as though the Dalek might continue with "Exterminate, exterminate." Using her card to pay, at least she could still see that, instead of cash that was fed into a slim gaping mouth and sucked into the bowels of the machine. It was nothing short of George Orwell's '*1984*'.

It had rained overnight rain to leave a clear blue sky and cool damp air. In the low morning sun the silvered road gleamed like brushed steel sockets on order for the kitchen. It was dazzlingly bright on the short journey to the pool.

Wednesday 12th September. She left a scribbled note leaning against her husband's mug by the kettle. "Have gone for fresh air will be back just after 10." Love JAx. Since the start of the day, high cloud had spilled over and blotted out the sun. It was often the way. By nine it was dull. The poplars shushed like the sea pulling on the shingle and it occurred to her as the willow branches rolled around in the wind and the slender leaves flipped over that the undersides were the exact colour of the Tiverton Grey cupboards being assembled in the kitchen. She walked around the edge of the field in the cool fresh breeze, dog walkers no longer bare armed but wrapped. She could see that with the hay cut and the trees starting to lose their leaves that it could be bleak, like a remote fen. No need to worry about not having a dog, a brown Labrador joined her for nearly a mile much to the annoyance of the owner who had to whistle several times to get the dog's attention. The haws, now ripe, flushed through the hedges. Still there were swallows flying low, but the magpies, crows and pigeons had more to say.

After five weeks the novelty of cooking in the field kitchen was wearing thin and reduced still further when the gas pressure lessened to such an extent that the single burner cooker was hurriedly set up to finish cooking the dinner. The evenings were drawing in and it was cooler.

There on the four pint milk bottle the use-by date was printed and served as a reminder of her son's birthday. Luckily until that day it hadn't rained. Setting up the kitchen in the porch instead, she attended to the food on her garden kneeler, rotating the pans until the celery soup, the chicken curry, and the rice were cooked and piping hot.

On Friday 14th September she swam her second mile.

A letter came in the post along with a contract to sign. Her third book, *Between the Stars* was going to be published. It hardly seemed possible. Never claiming to be an author she found it difficult to promote herself as such. To her and probably most, an author was someone fluent with words, brought up amongst literary academia, an elitist group fed and watered on the classics with whole walls devoted to books. Over a week after her son mentioned that his friend managed a book shop it dawned on her that he could be a useful contact and emailed him immediately. The success of her third manuscript had given her a buzz, enough to get her to local stores armed with some posters and a few copies to show. Ambitious, she started in Oxford. Along with the nose-to-tail peak-time traffic the bus slowly made its way along the shady leafiness of the Woodstock Road passed the mainly grand and imposing double fronted houses caught in the gentle variegated light.

Unlike the first assistant that she spoke to she felt that he wasn't really interested, his heart wasn't in it – unlike hers, beating madly beneath her ribs, palming her off with nothing more than an email address torn from a jotter and she let him get away with it. Her assertiveness that she had had only moments earlier drained away. She had wanted to show him her books and ask for them to be included in the stock, or to leave them by the tills for all to see, or have them included in the 'staff picks' selection, or simply to have them order ten of each and stack them on a display table for people to peruse and forget all about organising events, which seemed to her, the least favourite part of his job. She had wanted something confirmed, but the meeting at eleven was hastily concluded. Folding the piece of paper into quarters, she slipped it into the pocket of her bag. She had hoped for more. Arriving home she composed an email sending it out to the various branches of the bookshop chain. She didn't think much of emailing and saw it as a cop-out for the managers, a way of avoiding commitment and delaying making a decision. She had found this to be the case in the past, email replies were not forthcoming or at best the response was slow, ending up with her pestering with further reminders. Participating in a bookshop 'Event' was not about selling books, to sell one was a real achievement, but more about the ambiance and interaction with the public, looking again with fresh eyes and ears, looking beyond, learning something new. From her experience shops, particularly bookshops had become the new window shopping, browsing without buying, then returning home to fire-up the laptop and order on-line. The Internet was the demise of the bookshop.

As she knew they would be, the outcomes were varied. Doubting that the managers would go to the bother of checking the publisher's website her carefully worded enthusiasm would be deleted. Three days later, there were no replies. None came.

Tuesday 18th September. The brisk sharp wind filled the space around her and brushed the nap of the silky grass one way. Light spread over the field then withdrew as clouds spread through. The timid sun had lost its strength but she still felt its warmth on her back. A mewing sound caught her attention and looking up into the bubbling cloud she saw two buzzards spiralling high on the rising thermals.

Saturday 22nd September. She had made a cup of tea. The Battle of the Bulge was on television. "Where was the Battle of the Bulge?" Her husband asked her. Well she knew roughly. When the second cup of tea was requested, the 'please' thrown in as an afterthought, she stood and left the room, quickly changing her shoes and slipping on a jacket. He was indifferent and didn't give the impression that he cared if she went out or not. Calling goodbye, she stuffed her hands in her pockets and left him to watch the film. In the distance a full stop of a hot air balloon was drifting towards Northampton. Further, on the rise, three model plane enthusiasts, no two model plane enthusiasts and one mobility scooter were "looping the loop and defying the ground." There had been rain the night before. The crows cawed lazily in a nearby ash tree and the horses had their rugs on. The leaves were completely motionless. It was later than usual and the sun had spilled behind the flimsy cloud. A cat sat neatly on a wall, its paws tucked under watching her walk past, turning the corner, another crossed the road, her belly low to the ground with kittens. Arriving home, The Battle of the Bulge had ended. Hooray.

Sunday 23rd September. Lovingly, parents stood on the touchline sporting a colourful array of large umbrellas so that they could boast on Monday morning that Ben had scored the winner or swallow their pride and quietly mutter the eight nil defeat or sigh that they had drawn the short straw and got the filthy wet kit. It was raining and how it rained. From behind the door curtain she fetched her larger, with a slightly bent finial, slightly battered, older, no longer black umbrella that had a mind of its own, springing open fully as soon as the press-stud tab had been released. For ordinary walking it was fine or going to the library where she left it open outside with the dog bowl of water it was fine also, but for going to the newsagents or the butchers it had to be closed and fastened firmly and just for good measure she wrapped her hand round the canopy in case it launched into full sail. There was something primitive about an umbrella, like a tent or a shelter to protect against the elements. She took to Bury Field wearing her Barbour and her walking boots. The howling wind moaned in the trees and the persistent rain pushed and battered against the umbrella, sucking the fabric in and out like a flapping jib. Steely grey cloud hugged the ground. It was drab. There was nothing to commend the walk other than getting some fresh air and some exercise. Where the rain collected and dripped off the spokes of the umbrella her jeans were soaked and droplets of rain gathered in small pools in the folds of her sleeves. Unsettled, the crows fell about the sky. She ploughed along, her boots squelching in the surface water and the grass was sodden. Within six months, instead of walking 'round the block' walking round Bury Field had become her usual walk and she could vary it, lengthen it or shorten it according to time. She saw three people out walking their dogs, the last glad to get the dog walking job over and done with and she saw a couple standing close sheltering from the rain beneath a huge swaying umbrella of willow. Strewn around the goalposts where the boys had played football in the heat of the previous day on Riverside Meadow was an array of plastic bottles. Disappointing. Throwing rubbish down or simply leaving it was a pet-hate of hers, on a par with fly-tipping. In her head she would get on her soap box and launch an angry attack on the guilty culprits. There was simply no need.

Earlier in the morning she had been ironing. On the radio there had been a harvest festival service from the Parish Church in Cambuslang. In her head she sang along with the hymns. They reminded her of decorating and filling the recycled woven wooden punnets, used in those days for soft fruit often stained with bleeding juice, with fruit and vegetables or disguising a shoe box with crepe paper and making a mini-hamper. The children took it in turns to place their offerings into the hands of the vicar, who was like the Lord himself, who placed them carefully on the chancel steps. It was a special time and the church was beautifully decorated. It was like Christmas. Plain wooden sills were placed below the great Norman windows and arranged with apples entwined with garlands of hips and haws and old man's beard. Golden tombstones of autumn sun fell across the nave to the pews on the far side. Sheaves of wheat were propped against the font. "All is safely gathered in." It was like Bathsheba's barn in *Far from the Madding Crowd*. And then on the Monday evening she fondly remembered going to the harvest sale where all the produce not given to the needy, was auctioned off at inflated prices by Mr Ball, for the on-going church restoration.

Tuesday 25th September. It was warm, too warm for her jacket, but she had to put up with it, undoing the double ended zip. Dressed in less would not have been appropriate and remembered on a whale watching trip in the raw cold Atlantic, people meanly dressed for the conditions some wearing no more than flip-flops or a short sleeved shirt. Rugs covered the horses and they stood nibbling at the grass, their backs to the wind. With the wind for company the 180 acres was like a great lung of air, it buffeted her round the perimeter, it tugged and pulled, teasing at her hair until it escaped her collar, free to knot and tangle, knowing that she would wince later when she tried to comb it through. Swollen with wind, the trees roared, the branches twisted and turned, round and round relentlessly. Pushing through, great tumbles of cloud constantly rearranged themselves opening up patches of blue, letting in a blink of sun, then only moments later hiding it again.

Turning, she saw a flag of white tracing against the darkness of the trees, an egret making its way from the crashing weir just downstream, swallows darted silently, flicking around over the windswept grass.

When she parked in the Co-op car park she did not foresee the three car pile-up. At ten past five she placed the fish and chip suppers on the seat beside her, fastened her seat belt and checked her mirror. Behind her, out on her left was a beige coloured estate car, she could reverse straight back. As she did so however the beige metallic ghost appeared horribly close. Silently, it had rolled out of its parking space and was making its way across the car park at an acute angle to rest heavily against her nearside wing. She could feel the crushing pressure bearing down. Eventually the tensile strength of her blue Corsa succumbed and buckled under its sheer weight. Slowly she inched away and in disbelief she watched the unstoppable car come to a halt in the back of a black Seat. An onlooker who had observed the situation unfolding took a notebook from her cavernous bag and hastily made a note of the incident and the registration numbers. The owners of the runaway car were located at the nearby nursery; they appeared dismayed at the chaos in the car park. All the time she was thinking about her fish and chips getting cold with no means of warming them up.

On Friday 28th September she swam her third mile.

She enjoyed her day. It started with cleaning the kitchen windows followed by fastening a thin strip of sticky-backed foam to reduce the gale that entered via the frame and the glass. Then taking the step ladder to the big bay at the front of the house, she went up and down and on and off spraying each pane then buffing it with a soft cloth. It was precarious because the ladder only just fitted on the stretch of concrete below the window. Then she took a hand brush and brushed all the old blackened cobwebs that clung and hung to the boxed-in plywood ceiling of the porch along with the stubborn felting pupae, harboured for years and stuck fast in the corners. Then she removed the glass shade from the door light, washed it and screwed it back in place. She swept the step and picked up the rubbish that eddied in the corner. She had bought two trays of cheery pansies and filled a terra-cotta pot by the front door. Her husband had left her a trug of 'new' earth and she incorporated it with the existing compost and granules of plant food turning it thoroughly with her hand fork until it was a crumbly loam. Pressing the pansies carefully from the polystyrene tray with her thumb she positioned them round the edge of the pot, then sinking her fingers into the earth to make a little well she teased the roots of each pansy and popped them in, closing round with loose soil to finish. At the kitchen door she rearranged the assortment of pots and filled them, too, with pansies. High in the melting clouds she heard the mew of the buzzard. She cleared the rubbish that had accumulated at the kitchen door and in the afternoon sat with her book on a chair facing the sun.

The summer, for what it was, was quickly closing down. The need for sandals and cotton chintz dresses had gone. It was time to rearrange the wardrobe. Since finishing work there seemed no need for anything more than jeans and she had several pairs, courtesy of the numerous charity shops and one pair courtesy of a Marks and Spencer voucher. Everything remotely summery was removed from its hanger, folded and placed in an empty case. Some things had never been worn, some still lay on the bed in the spare room waiting to be hung up. Maybe next year she thought. All bar the suits the winter clothes were reinstated. As she removed the polythene covers she was reminded of her clothes once worn daily. Really she should make more effort to wear them. It was too easy to pull on the jeans.

It was 4am. She had lain awake since two, turning this way and that, listening on one side to her husband's ragged breathing and on the other to the persistent tick of the clock. Around the room familiar shapes were emerging. Around the edges where the curtain overlapped the track, the wall, and the sill it was a darker grey. The curtains had been slightly pulled apart and from the orange glow of the streetlamp a shaft of light fell over the wardrobe door. From her pillow she could only see the sky through the gap. Near the windowsill, in the distance there were strips of dawn light shading to grey nearer the ceiling. A telegraph pole on the other side of the road brought the phone cable to the house, dividing the sky at a jaunty angle. Although the windows were open, the curtains barely moved and for the time being the wind had loosened its grip. Breaking the silence, a blackbird sang at full throttle and a crow joined in with its deep ark. For a short time there was a fanfare of bird song. A car passed at 4.20am. It had been clean sheets night, her favourite and she breathed deeply the fresh intoxicating air on her pyjamas, brought straight from the line earlier in the day. What a marvellous smell.

Months soon slipped into one another and that wonderful, wonderful feeling of not going to work was as fantastic as ever. Sometimes a rush of blissful euphoria fell over her, a wave of guilty pleasure. Having the time, she had even taken to 'washing the nets' balling the socks and turning collars and like her fastidious neighbour, shaking a yellow duster or the bathmat from a bedroom window. She took to using handkerchiefs again, ironing them into quarters. There were odd moments when it seemed indulgent to stand and stare into space or look into the silence of empty rooms. She loved the solitude. With apparently nothing to do, she found herself looking out of the window over the garden to see the leaves shivering in the wind and the two CDs rocking and rolling on the apple tree, winking like a disco ball, oddly reflected in the trembling surface of the pond. But still she thought how truly wonderful. There comes a time when it is really time to stop. Not being governed by terms and timetables was liberating. Time took on a new dimension, determined by twice yearly dental appointments and quarterly bills that seemed to drop in with regularity, the swimming 'term session programme' 1st September – 26th October, the 'use-by' dates on milk, seeing the 28th when it's only the 16th, and egg boxes, seeing the 10th when it's only the 16th devoured whole weeks and of course the car tax. She did not wish for or long for or yearn for or hanker after what had gone by. Her timetable and names from her classes were fading fast from her memory.

There were some things that she missed. She missed the daily friendship of her two friends, the close bond that they shared. Sentences started and continued later when lessons had intervened, easy conversation about food, their children, going here and going there, following a series on TV, clothes, what they were reading, wondering what to make for dinner, going to the gym, booking the MOT and any general gossip. And that's all it was. But she liked their company. Over the years they had cried and laughed and been there for each other each step of the way. The break time coffee was made with the best of intention, however, more often than not the three cups were left to go cold. By one o'clock they ached to sit and sighed with relief when their behinds finally touched down, savouring the moment till one thirty and enjoying by then the much needed pot of tea and assortment of lunch time delicacies. They were so loyal and dependable. What more could you ask? Another thing that she found that she missed was the sense of pride in her class's achievements, especially when the twelve year olds made a set of quiches from scratch in just over an hour, filling the school with an inviting savoury smell, and the pupils the following week relaying their parents' comments and admiration. And over time she realized that she had lost the wealth of expertise that the staff in a large school could offer. Reluctantly she would have to source the internet for answers. Eventually she fell asleep.

It was the end of September. The moon stamped big mats of light on the floor. The night was still and she was wakeful, hearing people walking on the other side of the road, their voices fading to nothing. She lay for a long time, just lying still with her eyes shut, thinking, writing in her head, fretting about what shirt to wear, wanting to wear the collar fastened to hide the knotty gristly lumps that had appeared, a white shirt – always safe or the red checked shirt – although with jeans it had a bit of a cowboy look, or the paisley – that was a bit bulky and what jacket and what scarf and did she need a scarf or wondering wither to use the liver or the mince or get the chicken out of the freezer and make a curry?

In disbelief she looked at her watch. It had stopped at 6.51am and she missed the comforting reassurance of seeing its dependable second hand ticking round.

The woman coming down the stairs to the platform wore a bright sugar pink mac, belted and pulled tight at the waist over a badly washed grubby nondescript white knee-length skirt, flesh coloured tights and cowboy boots. She had a tight deceitful face and wore her blonde hair pulled up in a bun. Over her arm she carried a couple of roomy shopping bags, both light coloured, one with a pink sixties snowflake pattern on it and one with a scarf tied onto the strap. Nothing matched. She had an east European look about her and thought, taking in the sturdy legs, that she could have been a pole dancer. She followed her down two flights of stairs into the underground and on to the escalator.

For most of the journey the view scrolled past, she stared out the window holding a pen in one hand and a folded piece of paper in the other in case she had a thought. It was cool and still. The fields were ready for winter. Unconcerned about anything, horses, cattle and sheep kept their heads down, their fleshy lips slipping over their yellowing teeth, nibbling constantly. The chalk lion pale on the side of the Chilterns. Stopping at most stops, the train gradually filled up. As soon as people seated themselves, if not already in their hands, they whipped out their phones to text a message. 'I'm on the train.' Vapour trails criss-crossed the sky weaving skeletal remains, ancient fossils, blurry x ray images, wispy ribs and fragmented spines into a sinking downy web. Beyond, the silvery sun spread out. Fringes of gold edged the thin high clouds, and planes, a mile high, no more than a dash, were also brushed in gold, and for a moment the cockerel perched on the spire overlooking Bushey caught the light, glinted and was gone.

Arriving early she crossed into Trafalgar Square, ducked under the barrier around Nelson's Column and as though for good luck touched the front paw and the tail of a lion. Only the night before her husband had said. "Do you know why it is called Trafalgar?" No she didn't know why. The bronze lions, he explained, were made from the cannons salvaged from the ships of the defeated Spanish and French in the waters of Cabo Trafalgar. Walking back in the freshening breeze she went into Pret a Manger, bought a coffee and a tub of porridge and sat on a high stool overlooking St Martin's Place to wait for her son. Within moments he arrived, bringing with him a peal of bells as he pushed open the door, and his cheery personality. With tongue in cheek, she had suggested earlier in the week that he joined her for the service at 10 o'clock. Surprisingly he rose to the challenge. Being unfamiliar with the service she knew that he would be apprehensive. With a few minutes to spare, they took in their surroundings. On the periphery hunched over their lives, the dark cloaked shadows of hopelessness took shelter along the side lines, the simplicity of the chancel window, the ornate ceiling, and the congregation filing into the pews. The reading was about Esther and Mordecai and duly explained in the sermon. The gospel reading from Mark had everyone silenced, hanging on every word. "And if your eye causes you to stumble, tear it out; it is better for you to enter the kingdom of God with one eye than to have two eyes and be thrown into hell, where their worm never dies, and the fire is never quenched. For everyone will be salted with fire. Salt is good; but if salt has lost its saltiness, how can you season it? Have salt in yourselves, and be at peace with one another."

Afterwards, they took the tube to Highgate, laughing at the salt and the hell, the fire and damnation of it all. Continuing the religious theme, they went to Highgate Cemetery.

Loose soil slumped in the vague hollow spaces where the remains of the decayed and decomposing bodies once lay. Invisible. The sepulchres were like the people themselves, no two the same, all ages, all shapes and sizes, tilting and leaning, upright, collapsed and broken, drunken, crippled and deformed, humble, all-singing-all-dancing, like miniature marble houses with steps and a front door and windows to see out of. Encroaching ivy invaded, entwining through their lives, slowly strangling and choking them to death. In their haphazard way they stood in rows, threaded with narrow trampled paths, overrun with rabbits, urban foxes and prowling cats and overgrown and wild with scrubby weeds. Like sickening cancers, moss and lichens crept over and into the slabs of crumbling gravestones. Few were tended. Shady and cool beneath the ancient trees, as it had always been, the timeless monuments shared their secret wilderness with a canopy of birds and marauding squirrels.

Leaving in search of lunch they came across the Wrestlers, stoked with a warm friendly fire and a traditional Sunday roast. Looking at her watch, they shared the humour. It was 6.51am. Too quickly the day was slipping by. Pleasantly sustained they made their way over Hampstead Heath amongst the living; the kite runners, families out for a walk, lovers embracing, joggers and cyclists, to take in the sweeping view. In a great panoramic arc from east to west she took in the history that sprawled before her, recognizing landmarks and like others, pointing out the obvious buildings and views of the city. Tea and cake rounded off the day before hurriedly kissing her son goodbye, wishing him a happy birthday and a safe trip to Prague and making a dash for the train. Coming home it was overcast. The wind had got up. The horses, the cattle and the sheep had nibbled all day. They were still nibbling. The month ended neatly on a Sunday.

Big Ben struck six as she turned right to leave the multi-story car-park. It had been a day of ticking boxes, visiting places that she had been meaning to do for years but had never had the time.

7

Monday 1st October. Swallows still swept low over the grass. One day soon, she would look for them and they would be gone.

Taking the seat on the end opposite her Doctor's room she waited. With ten minutes to spare her Doctor arrived, opened her door and turned on the light. The door swung shut. She imagined her hanging her coat behind the door, firing-up the all-important computer and thinking about her day ahead while waiting for it to do so. In an effort to present a calming atmosphere, tinkling background music filtered from somewhere behind the ceiling and five framed prints, mounted on white and framed in black offered more than the blank wall facing her. A wall mounted screen flashed up information and advice. It wasn't level. At precisely 8.30am the door opened again. "Jane Burrr." Before she had finished she smiled, stood up and walked in. The door swung shut behind her. She was invited to sit and the two women exchanged pleasantries before she removed her scarf to show her, besides vanity, the reason for being there.

Always alert to what others might think and her own dislike of the two inflamed lumps, juicy and thriving, one more noxious than the other, that had erupted on her neck and bony chest. Like hard fatty tallow beneath a womb of thin transparent skin, pearly white embryonic pea sized nodules fed on wisps of blood, suspended in a watery sac. They hurt if she accidently knocked them and they looked disgusting. Enthusiastically the Doctor explained the risks, implying that lesions were fairly straight forward and the date was set for what she called a minor-op. Standing up to leave she wished her a good day and she reciprocated. Her first patient had come and gone.

During the night the one on her chest seeped and bled encrusting her pyjamas. It had changed, no longer pea shaped, more a black-eyed-bean shape and scabbed with pin-pricks of blood. Still disgusting, she covered it with a round plaster.

A month later she found herself sitting on the same chair opposite the same door and the same framed prints. The mood-music played. The appointment was for 8.30am and her Doctor entered her room at 8.25am. She was called into the treatment room where she removed her scarf and jacket and put her bag on the floor by the wall. After signing the form she leaned back against the pillow for the local anaesthetic. A neat square was cut in a green shroud and positioned over her. It took only moments to remove the sebaceous cyst. The cut was stitched and dressed and strict instructions not to get it wet advised. An appointment was organized for the removal of the stitches in a week's time. Slipping on her jacket, she picked up her bag and scarf and said goodbye. Five days later she removed the dressing.

In less than a week she was back. The Dr had phoned at 8.45am. In front of her she had the histology results of the cyst and started to explain what they meant. She could tell that that she found it too important to talk about over the phone and an appointment was made for later that morning. Carefully her mouth slipped over her teeth, explaining in detail that basal cell carcinoma was the least of the three skin cancers to worry about. Although her mind was awash, she did not feel worried. In a way she felt that she should be more so. The doctor thought that the bad news hadn't sunk in and that she needed time to think. In the meantime, an appointment with the dermatology specialist was organized.

A week later she sat waiting to be called. Overlooking Bury Field, dog walkers meandering the network of trodden paths. Immediately below, cars pulled in and out of the car park. Due to a change over in the computer system, the waiting room was quiet. Patients were being dealt with on a day-to-day basis and being put-off by the phone call procedure, enough to put anyone off being unwell, thus the lack of patients. The phone did not stop ringing. "We don't go live until next Wednesday." Said the receptionist as though a prime-time reality TV show was about to hit the screens. Glad to be escaping the launch of the new system she was waiting to see the nurse who was going to remove the three stitches from her neck. Removing her coat and scarf she sat and turned her head away.

It was the day of the icing on the cake; the arctic white fondant was perfectly formed and fitted over the cupboards and up the wall, the sink and the hob completed the streamline finish; her very own Taj Mahal. The manuals for the oven, the hob and the dishwasher lay open on the troubleshooting pages. The smooth clean lines off-loaded her mind of the busy grout between the tiles and the cement between the bricks that had been in place for so long. Loving the clear uncluttered surface she put nothing more than the toaster – the kettle – the pepper grinder and the stone wear pot of utensils on the worktop. She took the palm of her hand over it. The cool waxy feel was intoxicating. She took great pleasure in squeezing the soapy dishcloth tight and wiping in big smooth strokes and sweeping figure eights, gathering stray crumbs, then running the cloth around the edge of the sink and the edge of the hob, buffing the new tap.

On Friday the 5th of October she swam her fourth mile.

Keen to organise the cupboards she fitted the shelves and still in her pyjamas emptied the storage boxes which had served as cupboards for two months. No longer did she have to play slide puzzles with the tins and the mugs and the spices. At a glance she could see everything.

Anyone who came to the house was proudly shown the kitchen, flinging open the soft close doors and drawers to show them where everything was housed. The under the sink cupboard contained the usual things plus the bin and the compost tub. In the next cupboard on the top shelf were all the glasses and below, the big serving dishes and platters. The corner cupboard contained all the casserole dishes, coffee pots, jugs, and cake tins that were not in use and, most importantly, her cook books, the smaller ones on a little wooden bookshelf that her husband made at school, and the bigger ones leaning against the side of the cupboard and propped with a stack of magazines. The next was what she called the everyday cupboard for tea and coffee, cereal, marmalade, bread, love-it-or-loath-it Marmite, oil, wine, if there was any, cod liver oil capsules and cake tins that contained something interesting like some coconut rock cakes or a Bakewell tart. Then there was the oven then in the next cupboard were the tins and dry ingredients, pasta and rice and the flours and the baking ingredients. Couscous, and basmati and oats and pudding rice were decanted into Dartington glass storage jars. In the four drawers at the end were the paracetamols and the Lem-sips, then the cake decorations, then the herb and spice jars, then the tin foil, cling film and sandwich bags.

Wednesday 10th October. There were no signs of swallows. Their epic journey had begun. She had underestimated how much it had rained. Brooks feeding the river had reappeared, puddles lay. The river was brimming. Leaves had started to fall to float on the surface. There was a smell of autumn. It took a moment at the third stile to work out where she would put her feet. It looked for all the world like a herd of cattle had partied. Slipping her voice recorder into her pocket so that it didn't fall, she negotiated the slopping mud. Once into the field a herd of cattle grazing in the far corner confirmed the cause. They ambled slowly towards the gate, the gate that she needed. Back-tracking, she took herself to the first stile to start her walk again.

Thursday 11th October. As the forecast promised, it started to rain. The drizzle crescendo increased to strikes of rain coming down aslant. She didn't mind the dull hollow sound of the pattering rain on the umbrella. She felt safe. It was comforting and dependable, its steady monotony almost therapeutic. The sullen sky was full of weather. A veil of low cloud grudgingly hung over her walk. Before slipping between the two gates, she returned a book to the library, stopped off at the cash dispenser, made an appointment at the hairdressers for Saturday and one at the beauticians for Friday. The rain eased.

Sunday 14th October. Before leaving she consulted the oracle, her husband, checking when it would become dark. Pushing her hands deep in her pockets she walked briskly determined to reach the far corner of the field, turn and walk back before it was dark. It was five past six. A huddle of dog walkers had gathered to chat at the end of their walks. It was a still cool evening. The light was sombre and failing quickly. In the distance she could see the darkened shapes of people still walking their dogs and model aeroplane enthusiasts still flying their planes, making the most of Sunday. Turning just before the far gate she made her way back, the lights of the town visible over the brow of the rise. With the crows roosting, only the sound of her boots thrusting through the grass disturbed the quiet. The haunting pale sweep of the barn owl stopped her in her tracks. The enfolding darkness reminded her of walking with her son in the Lake District, of coming down from Black Sail Pass towards Buttermere in the vanishing light, her stomach a riot as she slipped on the scree slope. Approaching the jagged outline of the High Street, the lights brought an early darkness.

Seeing the end of the kitchen project in sight, she went off to check-out the log burners. The gas pipe to the dining room fire was capped. Coming in from swimming on Wednesday her husband had started to dismantle the fireplace. The hearth was particularly stubborn to dislodge and heavy. The sack barrow was wheeled in to transport it outside. A trip to Browns in Leighton Buzzard to buy a chain-saw brought a whirl of activity. Her husband launched into splitting and cutting logs, worshipping them like standing stones as he gathered and grouped them in the sun to dry off, stacking them and storing them in what they called the 'wood shed' to season. He logged the logs in his diary. To see how much moisture was lost he weighed a log and made a note, checking it a week later, it had lost a pound. "A pint of water weighs a pound and a quarter." He trilled. Saw dust clung to his socks and he traipsed through the house shedding what looked like rolled oats all over the floor. She cleared the sodden bark to the dump. The novelty of collecting logs never wore off. Sometimes they were buried in leaf litter, mossy with age, lodged in the undergrowth or wedged in the mud. However they were, he pulled and levered and lifted them until they were free. Nothing pleased him more than the back of the Land Rover piled with logs and he was quickly frustrated if unable to gather them to feed the ferocious appetite of the wood burner. When they were out and about he drooled over logs abandoned to the elements, and almost wept when a felled tree was fed into the shredder.

On the success of removing the hearth into the garden, they tidied-up and went off to Emberton Park, her husband to fish and for her to read and walk and stride into Olney for fish and chips.

Little shoals of leaves played, constantly moving the golden carpet at the entrance to the park. It was a bright blousy day, broken cloud swept through, overtaking and overlapping, casting alternate lightness and darkness over the ground when it hid the sun. The wind tore at the leaves whipping them into a frenzy, laughing all the time they scurried this way and that to gather and drift against the wall or collect along the gutter. The wind in the trees roared like the sea, the higher branches bending and swaying, the stouter ones producing high pitched squeaks like the sound of violins striking-up as they rubbed together. The wind zipped over the grass. Crows dragged themselves around. Gulls circled and cried forlornly. Arguments broke out between the ducks; none would back down, each wanting the last quack. Any noise was drowned out by the tumbling waves in the trees. Like moire taffeta the windswept lake shimmered, catching the light, forever shifting. Little gusts of wind stirred the reeds and wrinkled the water constantly. All the time petals of gold spiralled and fluttered to float on the dancing surface. Furled sycamore leaves bobbed like a flotilla of ducklings. Shadows lengthened in the low autumn sun.

When the weather was suitable and the wind was right her husband occasionally went fishing for one or two nights, leaving her to her own devices. As always his presence interrupted her train of thought. Without the distraction she had sense of freedom. Not having to consider anyone but herself, she wallowed in the endless time, filling the day. Like a chalk outline in a crime scene or the recovery position she luxuriated across the entire bed completely motionless. Unlike the normal riot of covers in the morning the bed didn't look slept in and she could tell by her ruffled eyebrow that she hadn't slept on her usual side. She would sneak a shallow bath and sit up in bed with the light on, or put the light on during the night, or take her breakfast upstairs and listen to the radio. She would read and write in bed. Curled on the sofa, she watched TV programmes that since the onset of Sky Sports, she had lost touch with. She only spoke when she was on the phone or when out and about. She didn't close the doors and the house streamed with light. Eating amounted to grazing, a packet of boil in the bag kippers, mainly because they had reached their use-by-date, a bowl of soup, a banana, nothing that took any time. She gardened and swam and went for walks. On her own she tackled jobs that she delayed doing when her husband was about, things that were noisy or irritating to him or things that needed a long uninterrupted time for her, tidying the bookshelf or emptying the drawers or vacuuming behind the bed. After swimming she took the home-alone opportunity to make her kitchen door curtain. In the kitchen she set up the ironing board and transported her sewing machine downstairs, along with her scissors, pin box, threads and tape measure. With the radio for company it took several hours to complete, stopping briefly for a three course lunch of a yogurt, liver (these too had reached their use-by-date) and onions and cabbage, and another bowl of borscht. Why does the programme 'A Good Read' not feature new authors? She put away the ironing board and returned the sewing machine back upstairs and hung the new curtain over the banisters. Putting on her jacket and lacing her boots she went out for a walk. A light breeze brushed the grass and disturbed the trees. Excitable dogs took their desk bound owners out for some fresh air. Facing the sun, everything was black and she remembered driving down Silver Street, the welding white light of the same sun literally stopped her in her tracks. Unable to see anything she levered herself from her seat to duck behind the mirror and hide behind the visor. Once home, she made a large cup of tea while she emptied the dishwasher. Already thinking about the next day she weighed ingredients for apple scones and a flapjack. Immersing the shower head in the kettle, she descaled both and gave all the plugholes a dose of soda crystals sluiced down with boiling water. She listened to the radio into the evening. The whole house was quiet, no TV, no closing doors, no sighing, no complaining at the TV, no irregular breathing and no snoring through the night.

A faint glow radiated from the turning leaves, lighting up the drab October day. The sky was thick and murky, the air smelled damp. Not even the lightest leaves of the bamboo murmured. Nothing moved. Unable to dry out, the ground was wringing wet.

On Friday the 19th of October she swam her fifth mile.

Saturday 20th October. The wealth of a bottle of wine drew her out for a walk via Bargain Booze, the long way round. It was a pale high sky and the model plane enthusiasts were out in force. In view of doing the circular walk, not tackled for a while she wanted to see if the cows were in the field and took to the narrow lane. Since she last walked, it had been cut back, opening up the track, letting in the light, it was grassy and although muddy in places, it was easy to navigate round the puddles. On reaching the gate she could see that once again it was flooded, the lakes spilling over into one another. Her feet squelched through the waterlogged grass. Where the water flooded over the path she stopped. In the distance she could see the cows, idly following one another.

Turning, she made her way back. 'The autumn leaves were turning to the colour of her hair.' As the chlorophyll faded from them, ochre flames flared through the spicy browns, the tawny and blazing copper, the fiery russets and smouldering berry shades. Haws braided and draped themselves through the tweedy hedgerow; along with scattered splashes of orange hips they garnished the dark dying undergrowth. Their small convex windows of light gleamed in the low pallid sun melting through the thinning leaves. When they could no longer hold on, tears of gold gently pattered to the ground to curl and decay. Golden pools lay below the trees.

It was the day of ticking boxes. Her friend had a great desire to go to a pie and mash shop and to savour again the childhood memory of cockles and whelks. They did both, starting in Borough with a cup of coffee generously laced with illicit brandy, secreted from the bottom of her bag. Having stood on trains for almost two hours, the sit down was welcomed as was the intoxicating warmth of the coffee. With map in hand the three friends walked along Great Dover Street, kicking through the dunes of fallen leaves to Manze's in Tower Bridge Road, London's oldest pie and mash shop. They stepped into another era. The original art nouveau green and cream tiles still graced the walls, and wooden benches lined the weighty slabs of marble that formed the tables. Just inside the door they queued and ordered their food. The mash was liberally scraped to the side of the plate, the pie and the eel to the side. Over it all, a ladle of liquor, an insipid lucid sauce flecked with parsley. Never had she seen such a plateful of unappetizing bland food. The smell was not to be recommended either. Slipping along the bench she put her thoughts aside and set to, carefully removing the slimy skin from the discs of eel and picking her way round the spine. Years ago the bones would have been spat into the sawdust covered floor. To the eel she added a little mash and some liquor. Mmm, yummy. She took in her surroundings. The shop was busy, the turnover rapid and she noticed that customers dowsed their food with vinegar and pepper. I wonder why, she thought. With what little mash she had left, she reached for the seasonings. Not surprisingly there was an improvement. Washing their food down with Zasparella, a drink as alien to her as the food they had just eaten, they cleared their plates and left. It was a bit of a trek but as it was still early she suggested going to see her son's art work that was still showing at Hubbub on Westferry Road. Sharing a bottle of house red they looked over the pictures and laughed over the miss-pronunciation of Chanel as channel. And it was funnier still when they stood on the corner and consumed their cockles and whelks – again dowsed with vinegar from Tubby Isaac's seafood stall – that at the bottom of their polystyrene cups was an inch of sandy eau de channel. They crossed the road, their gritty mouths wrung of sea-water, nothing that a couple of bottles of Merlot couldn't put right and they settled by the window until peak time travelling was over.

Seeing a weed between the slabs was as bad as a crumb or a bit of fluff on the carpet. It had to be removed

She would make a cup of tea and take it outside to drink when she thought about it. While pulling on her perishing rubber gloves and fastening her knee protectors tightly she would have a couple of sips then more often than not, forget all about it, returning an hour later to find it stone cold. On her hands and knees she pulled weeds and cleared last year's leaves from beneath the hedge. As she filled one trug, she fetched another, slowly making her way along the path to the new garden, fenced to the boundary but as yet un-gated. Her husband had big ideas – apple trees – an asparagus bed – two vegetable plots. Firstly the new garden was cleared of rubbish, things stored out of sight never to be used again and the shed was collapsed and left while the new footings were constructed and levelled from the rubble of the kitchen. Then the base was set on a raft of slabs, the sides re-assembled and a new roof felted and battened into place. Acquired from their neighbour, the sizable garden brought with it a burst of excitement for her husband, who loved planning and deciding what to grow. He revelled in the back-aching digging and would not hear of hiring a Rotavator. The more labour intensive the better, thriving on the strenuous work of it all. The new garden required nourishment and for countless hours they took themselves off in the Land Rover to collect sacks of well-rotted manure. Her husband backed up the Land Rover towards the haunch of manure. Removing his shoes, he pulled on his boots and set to, slicing into the rich seam with the spade, admiring the decomposed quality and the sheer weight of it, he levered and lifted and twisted. Like the digging it was back breaking. Rubber gloved she held open the flopping sack, adjusting the weight each time a spade of manure was added. While still manageable, but only just, her husband took hold of the sack and with a hefty heave swung it into the back of the Land Rover and she unfolded and positioned another. Over a couple of weeks her husband logged and tallied the number of sacks, so that he would know for next year.

Several years ago she had bought a machine to vacuum the leaves in the garden. Having not used it for a year her husband had threaded a length of wood through the handle and suspended it completely out of reach on the rafters of the garage. Placing the step ladder beneath, she eventually prised it from its support. God it was awkward and she quickly understood why it had been hung out of reach. She could see no reason why it had to be so cumbersome and unwieldy. In a garden littered with obstacles, like steps and logs and flower pots, keeping an eye on the trailing cable and holding the bulky apparatus was exacting. It didn't help either that she was running out of time and would have to put it away before going for her one forty five appointment. The speed of clearing the leaves, however, more than made up for the aesthetics and its offensive industrial drone. Within minutes she had made an impression. Like the mice, there would be casualties. A shiny dark green frog lay in the gravel by the path. After passing it a few times its position remained the same. Scooping him up she popped him in trug bound for the garden waste bin at the dump. At a furious pace she walked into town. In the calm warm sanctuary of Lifestyle, Eve took her jacket and hung it on the back of the door. Slipping out of her shoes she lay down on the narrow towel-covered bed freshly laid with tissue.

Returning to the garden an hour later it began to rain and curtailed any further activity.

The salon had had a makeover. Other than a whole wall racked and devoted to bottles of shampoo, sprays, serums and solutions to solve any of life's little problems, the salon had been painted deep purple. Elaborate rococo style mouldings and decoratively carved chairs and mirrors were sprayed silver, and the button backed chairs and the settee in the waiting area were upholstered in silver. Flat screens blasted out the sounds.

"As soon as I saw it, she said, I thought, dust. "

"That never occurred to me." He said.

No, she thought, it wouldn't. "Do you have a little slave with nimble fingers, a tooth brush and a feather duster?" She continued, saying that she had already been that morning to the local hospice shop with a box of clutter that required constant dusting. There was no reply to that, but overhearing the conversation, another hairdresser couldn't help laughing.

"Can I ask you to stand up?" It was normal for her to stand for a haircut and Lee divided her scalp into sections, dully cutting two inches off, then turning her to face him, he levelled the front and dried it off.

It was the time of year. Less than a week later the leaf sweeper was out again.

She raked the fallen leaves and windfall apples. She swept the path and took the three trugs of green waste to the dump.

The sun cut through the motorway traffic and glinted on the screens. The reason for the journey was an invitation to her friend's daughter's hen party. These parties had become standard procedure in the run-up to the big day. She had never been to one. Altogether there were nineteen guests. Apart from the bride to be, who wore turquoise sequins, wearing black was requested. The first activity planned was an Italian meal, where sashes and novelties were handed out and the hen wore the tiara and netty veil. She was happy to sit and talk, sip, eat and observe the scene and it was over too soon. On mass they moved to the next venue, a cocktail bar, where the music was loud and not what she knew, mini drinks chosen from an extensive menu and served six at a time in little recessed trays and downed as a dare, then on to an eighties club to dance. All the time the sylph like friends took pictures of each other on their iPhones, recording the event, their slim and smooth toned arms outstretched, bling rattling on their wrists, artistically holding and pressing the buttons one handed, then stroking the screen and showing what they had just taken to each other. Even dancing they held their conch shaped bags in one hand and their iPhones in the other.

8

Taking the stairs to level 4, she gave her name and time of her appointment to the receptionist, who in turn apologized for the computer not being up and running, jotting her name on a piece of paper. She took a seat in the designated area and sat taking in the grim cross-sections of cancerous growths depicted on the posters. Within moments she was handed a dermatology questionnaire fastened to a clip board to fill in while she waited. The questions, like most on questionnaires were black or white. It asked about blistering. Into her mind came the hot summer of 1959, when she was eight, her forehead and shoulders blistered and peeling. Living from hand-to-mouth as they did, sunscreen was ill-afforded. Sun-bathing was like smoking, nobody knew that there was anything to worry about. Well no, she didn't remember blistering in recent years. She ticked the no box. She loved being out in the sun and took every opportunity to be so. When holidaying abroad she applied sun-screen but in England she rarely bothered, she was so rarely out in the sun for any length of time. And now retired and able to go out every day, she looked forward to an all-the-year-round wind-blown weathered complexion. It was cruel to be deprived of that feeling of wellbeing that a sun warmed skin gave her, to be deprived of what it represented, relaxation, time, freedom, affluence. Besides her, two other women sat, waiting to be seen, one had come with a friend and they talked feverishly about food and furnishings. The Dr looked at her lesions with a hand held ultrasound device. Indeed there were cancerous cells.

She drew his attention to the suppurating lesion that had burst and two others that had appeared on her shoulder. He said that being fair skinned, they were suspicious and advised keeping an eye on them and to stay covered up and wear a broad brimmed hat in the sun.

Although now a faded marmalade colour, her once auburn hair had been rich and conker shiny and apart from the flaccid eggshell-coloured inside-arm skin, as pale as the underbelly of a tortoise or a snake, she had never known herself to be without freckles. It was hard to think that the sun had found a spot to damage between the sheltering overhanging crag of chin and her swinging hair.

On the surface she took it in her stride. She was indifferent, almost blasé. Over and over she said to those who asked that she was fine or okay, when all the time she was not. She did worry. Maybe the itching, endured for years, had not been eczema after all. Without warning when her skin flared she was alert, it was itchy and she scratched for relief. Her imagination quickly spiralled out of control. Into her mind came a web of fetid bloodied rhizomes and gristly fibrous knots burying insidiously below the epidermis, spreading their inflamed tentacles to erupt into scabrous septic masses. She could see that over time her body would be mutilated with scarring. Daily there were freckles to check and itches to calm, moles to keep-an-eye-on. While it was dull with winter it was not a problem but with the onset of warmer days she knew that she would long to be free of basting herself in thick greasy creams and covering up with sleeves. Sometimes her husband said, "Go and put some shorts on, or a skirt." And although she did, she thought, what's the point? And she was sad. Inside she was saying, 'why me?' and took to looking at other people the same age as her, people with visible blemishes, lesions and moles, 'why not them?' It was a wake-up-call.

Closely linked to food was shopping for it. Shopping was like breathing and though at times she tried not to, it had to be done, there was no avoiding it. No longer needing to go when the supermarket was at its zenith, shopping was still not a day out experience but fitted into the day in the minimum amount of time possible. Along with millions of others, she too, although usually a savvy shopper, was being forced to make further economies all round in an effort to reduce the length of the till receipt. Only the other day a woman in front of her did not have enough money to pay for her shopping and had to keep returning the items until the total equalled that of the contents of her purse. Dismayed, she said several times as she passed back the tinned tuna, the jar of jam and the box of juice to be scanned and invalidated that she hadn't bought anything. In leaps and bounds the prices spiralled, not just 2p here 2p there but 60p, 38p, 45p, the increases were massive. Then she'd notice that the very same product had a yellow 'price drop' sticker. The own brand olive spread was a £1 instead of £1 39p, nearly 25% reduction. So what was the price? Double cream, her favourite, was the same price as single. It had never been the same price. And they sneakily reduced the weight but retained the price. She could go on and on. A box of own brand malted wheat was £1 19p, three weeks ago it was more but in her local coop their own brand malted wheat was more than twice the price for half the amount. Hoping to shop locally regularly, she had gone to great lengths to having her bicycle adapted to allow her to carry heavy things like milk and tinned tomatoes without crashing into the curb or swerving into the road. One evening when her husband was away and she took command of the remote controls, she watched a programme called Scrimpers, a series about giving practical tips and advice about being more economical. Tea taste-testing was carried out and the tea that was the winner with the builders was Tesco's value brand. Its strength and colour was superb. Always on the look-out for a bargain she bought a box and decanted it into her Victorian tea chest. Accidently forgetting to admit to her husband that there had been any change in brand, he was non-the-wiser and she was a whole £2 richer.

Her Tesco Clubcard vouchers had come in the post along with a set of money-off coupons. With these and a £5 Helping Hand Coupon from last week to return to the store if she spent more than £40 she pared her bill by £18. "I don't blame you."

said Linda at the checkout. It was quiet in the store. Linda continued. "You should have been here on Wednesday, it was like Christmas. It was packed. Peter Andre was here signing his CD." Nodding in agreement, even though she didn't know who Peter Andre was, she said. "Well I write books and I'd get about two people." Suddenly she was more than interested and rummaged below the counter for something to write on. Producing the cardboard back off the pad of luggage vouchers, she passed it to her along with a pen to jot down the titles, actively involving the next customer waiting in the queue.

There was an eager edge to the wind. The sky was keen and sharp. The sun offered no warmth and settled for most of the day just above the rooftops. Distorted shapes leapt strangely over the garden, silhouetted against the brightness, the washing pole stabbed long and thin and the clematis covered trellis stretched forward like a high black wall. In the sun the leaves glowed.

Had she not got up she would have missed the lemon slice of silver moon. It was a dark morning and really it was too early to get up. But she had had enough of lying down. If she lay too long on her back she generated too much heat and too long on her side, her shoulders and ribs, where the pressure on her starving bones felt sore. No, she was glad to be up, away from the merging dreams.

It was not unusual to wake in the night. Feeling overly hot, she would throw off the weight of covers and sandwich her arms round the coolness of the pillow and stretch out her feet to the furthest cotton corners of the bed, until the uncertain clammy feeling subsided. Until she fell asleep again, she used this wakeful time to think and write in her head. Outside the traffic hissed passed in the rain.

Her nights were sometimes busy and she would wake feeling tired exhausted from her dreams. Her consciousness fought to hang on to the dream before it escaped her. She had been in the rambling house before in another dream. *Walking in she found her grown-up son and his friends having a watch party and all around clever lighting illuminated sparkling and glamorous designer watches displayed in little glass dishes. The party goers were clean cut with their hair slicked back, ties knotted, their double breasted suit jackets buttoned, like gangsters. Picking up his baby brother to comfort him she undid the door into the house that had been left derelict. Feeling her way, yet it was not dark she put him down and he started to crawl. A plank of wood became dislodged and he dropped through. She went to move but her weight imbalanced everything. In slow motion a great tumbling started. Through and through she went, her son just ahead of her in his turquoise towelling Baby-grow.* Beside her, her husband was saying "It's alright, it's alright."

Drowsing just below sleep she heard conversations carried on the still night air. Someone late home ran along the road. *With unsettledness brought dreams of wallpaper, rucked and blistered from dampness, torn and hanging from the walls.*

They were back where they used to live. Children were playing in the street. She accepted the job at the school. The interview was held at the doctor's surgery. All he did was take her personal details and while they were there they registered with the surgery. Moments later while waiting at the bus stop it occurred to her that she didn't know what she was going to teach. Going back, it was to teach in a middle school. "But I can't do maths." She implored, insisting that she only taught technology. He implied that she had had all summer to learn. Relieved, she was glad to wake up.

She was back where she lived as a child at a house that she knew. Leaning against the wall was an old black bike. She went to move it and as she did so, simultaneously the handlebars lifted from the stem and the top of the saddle came off to reveal a saddle full of rubble. Like a marionette the whole bike collapsed to the ground.

Eventually falling asleep in snatches, *she was walking, inappropriately dressed near the Thames, in the distance the city and beyond, the estuary. The ground was low-lying, sodden, waterlogged in places and even though only a few inches deep, a small bolder moved and she felt as though she was slipping in. No.*

The remains of a meal lay unfinished on the table, the dishes unwashed. Frightened, she crouched down beside her baby son under the table trying to pacify and sooth him. On the verge of ... She could not recall.

The man sat at the bar with a lacerated ear. His other ear was misshapen and looked like a question mark. To this man's head two others screwed a piece of wood. And the woman he was with, although she looked quite normal from the front, when she turned she had a deformed bottom literally like two plums and then the man who walks his dog past the house most days offered her a drink and almost passed it to her before withdrawing it and drinking it himself from a silver chalice.
Sometimes she revisited dreams like *the one with the very large barn shaped house built on a great grassy mound at the other end of town. Around the table in the dining room were at least forty people were sharing a meal, talking and laughing. She slipped out unnoticed to find herself in a nearby mill stream, thunderous water pressing her below the surface. She was gasping and frantic in the rush of water, trying to regain her breath.* Her agitation woke her husband, blissfully asleep beside her. "It's alright, it's alright."

Sunday 4th November. All morning it had rained cold wet rain. From the east it had splattered against the front windows. Not a day to venture out but by four it had eased and she resurrected a hat and gloves, wrapped-up warmly and took herself out for a walk. Navigating the puddles she walked round Riverside Meadow, crossed Tickford Street and into Castle Meadow. Crossing the foot bridge she turned into the graveyard. The river was swollen with brown rolling water, eddying and churning, twigs and crests of debris surged along. Alerted by the shrill whistle she stopped. Turning, she saw the turquoise jewel, travelling low, straight and fast downstream. A flash of azure iridescence dazzled the drab Sunday afternoon. Settling quietly on an overhanging branch, with a backdrop of turbulent water, it was pure theatre, drama at its best. A little treasure of a bird, he made a dashing spectacle, his neatly chiselled shape, his intense colours, his pointed beak, a shimmering gem. Seeing the kingfisher was a rare and special moment, she felt immensely privileged. Silver beads dripped from the leaves.

Monday 5th November. During the night the sombre cloud had lifted. All day the sky was clean. Posting a letter she continued into Bury Field. In the distance where it had trespassed over and into the field silvery edges fringed the river. With most of the leaves dispersed the bare bones of trees were black against the sky. Ahead, everything was black, even the Golden Labrador fetching the ball was black. Turning away from the sun, she could see again. Without a care finches scooped about.

Tuesday 6th November. Needing to change her repertoire of walks and one that was away from the continual effects of flooding, she told her husband that she was going to do the Willen Lake walk, a man-made walk which apart from bikes avoided the traffic and was mud-free, walked many times with her son but not alone. Thinking he would say, "I don't really want you walking round there." He said instead. "Don't talk to strangers." Strangers were the least of her thoughts. Having his blessing however made the walk entirely manageable. It did not enter her head that she could be mugged on a secluded path, like the reports she read about in the local paper from time to time. Where they hadn't plastered themselves to Tongwell Lane, the brown dying leaves mulched where they fell and drifted. Spindly nettles leaned towards the light where the overhanging trees had not met. It was almost rural. As always though, the thrum of the motorway, along with that of the bypass crowded out the sound of the birds busy fluttering back and forth in the undergrowth, the sound of the wind in the trees and the babbling stream that ran alongside the narrow lane. Then, further on, the landscape workers were cutting back and coppicing overgrown shrubs and feeding them into the shredder, decanting the woodchips back to the ground. The strong vermillion whips of dog-wood warmed. It occurred to her as she walked through the landscaped areas that somewhere in the vicinity there should be name plaques to inform young people about the names of the trees, because quite honestly most called a tree a tree or a bush a bush. With ash die-back making the headlines, the Times brought out its own tribute The Great British Tree Guide pull-out. Her boots pressed into the acorns that the squirrels had missed. There were people about, a couple of runners stretched out in Lycra, two men, en route to work on their bikes, a gaggle of walkers, a mixed bunch, a young couple hugging their lattes and a few single women, like her out for a walk. Ducks, she knew the mallards and a pochard, other than that she didn't really know about ducks, but there were ducks worth sighting, one man held up his binoculars. She didn't know the winter visitors, or the migrants. She could identify grebes, coots and moor-hens. Caught up in the wind, the lakes were choppy, gulls squawked, swooped and circled, dipping into the water. She knew even less about gulls. A fleet of swans bobbed on the silvery surface. At half-time she ate the much needed segmented orange and wizened apple, peeled and quartered, lurking in a plastic bag in the depths of her pocket. When she was working, she dreamed of taking walks, wrapped-up against the cold.

Wednesday 7th November. There was a tension in the house. Her husband was in plumbing mode. From the loft to the garage the whole house was affected. A thin plastic tube spiralled from the loft hatch, draining the tank into a bucket perched on a dining room chair, the aluminium ladder leaned against the banisters, the airing cupboard door was open and the ironing board discarded, the carpet was prised from the gripper in the bathroom in order to get at the pipes, all the doors were open. On and off his knees, his breath laboured. There was much sighing. Like his mother, he was easily stressed and as soon as one problem was solved he lurched to another. Making herself scarce, she sat hiding at the computer for a couple of hours, then weighed the rice, prepared the curry and went out for a walk. Although sometimes reluctantly, around four the dog walkers were out in force, anxious that their beloved pets exercised before flopping down in their baskets or curling-up beside the fire for the day, ultimately feeling pleased with themselves and benefitting from the effort. On her return, with the worst of the plumbing over, her husband had had a new lease of life. The urgency to re-install the radiator in the kitchen meant that the wallpapering had to start in earnest. Quickly the kitchen table was cleared and the paste mixed in a washing up bowl. Once the first length was pasted to the wall, they were away, her husband on the chair holding the top, her taking the roll towards the skirting and marking with a pencil, returning the roll to the table, cutting the length, pasting liberally, pasting the wall liberally then transferring the length from the table to the wall, matching the green maple leaf motif, smoothing and trimming. And so it continued until Sunday. Before being covered forever, her husband dated the wall 10/11/12 DULL, 11/11/12 SUNNY. With limited paper, there was no room for manoeuvre. They would have to accept mistakes. It was a testing time, estrangement a breath away. Surely no-one could wallpaper together and not be truly devoted.

For most of the uneventful journey she played with her camera, looking at the pictures still not downloaded and needing the space to take more, deleting those which no longer held her interest. Aiming for Charing Cross Road first, she took the Northern Line. She liked to think that where the gap leaned next to Clockwork Orange was where her book had been and imagined a customer browsing and coming across a 'new' author. Objectively she picked up a book set at an angle on the display table that had been recently reviewed in the weekend papers. On the back it gushed with its merits. She was in the store to ask about her books but hadn't the courage. Assistants were few and far between and they looked the same, small, brisk and confident, the men bearded and efficient, could locate any book in the universe with the touch of a key.

Would they take her seriously? She went to the café, off the cookery section, to think. Along with her mug of coffee she would have liked something to eat, but it was grossly overpriced. The spacious area had a worn comfortable ambience, a familiar old fashioned charm and once seated, it was hard to get up and leave. Like a church hall, it was full of pews and random church chairs, and rustic tables of varying sizes. A row of tall stools overlooked Charing Cross Road or rather T K Max. Jazz filtered quietly through the sound system. Slipping from her stool, she sat instead facing the room. About twenty people were scattered, reading, talking, using their laptops, checking their texts, passing the time of day. They sat for ages, way past the tables being cleared. On the strength of the coffee she asked at the till near the main entrance if either of books were in stock. The assistant's eyes scanned the monitor from side to side. Neither were in stock nor had they been. Yet she had sent copies more than eighteen months ago and it was implied that they had been despatched to the relevant departments and absorbed into the stock. In that time she had been in the bookshop a couple of times and assumed that the absence of the titles meant as she thought now, that they had been sold. Initially she was disappointed, then incensed, annoyed at being deceived, led to believe that they were genuinely interested in her work and in her. Behind the patronizing smile, there was a vulgar leer of distain. Feeling grieved, let down and excluded, as though what she had written was not worth reading about, she felt that she had been fobbed off. Their elitism was exactly what her books fought against. Trembling, she thanked the assistant and returned to the underground. Thinking later, she was not naïve. She knew that food was adulterated and clothes cut and pinned to make them look good. And they too had palmed her off anxious to clear the store of her clap trap and get on with serving real customers. The drizzle developed. The trees along the Embankment offered some shelter against the steady rain. Turning off she walked via Temple, St Pauls and on to Monument, built to commemorate the Great Fire of London by Sir Christopher Wren, climbing over three hundred steps to take in the views. The brown river ran towards the sea. Landmarks dissolved into the pewter sky. The man standing next to her on the tube fed the steaming hot pasty up the paper bag towards his mouth, biting into it with relish. It smelt good. Her mouth filled with saliva. It was her intention to have lunch and she could not remember a time when she had eaten on her own, usually making do with a coffee or a sandwich or nothing at all. She had lunch overlooking Euston Road just across from the station where the buses pulled out. She had about an hour and ordered a glass of red wine and spaghetti carbonara from the menu, partly because her husband was not a lover of creamy sauces and therefore she rarely made it but mainly because she really liked it. A wall of glass brought a mute scene. Outside it was raining, people hurried by, their umbrellas up, leaves spiralled constantly and in an effort to keep the gutters clear, a road sweeper cruised the kerbs. The pasta was good but she knew that the salty pancetta would later bring on a raging thirst. She ordered a coffee. Company would have brought a lingering finish to the meal. Instead, she paid the bill, zipped up her jacket and stepped out into the closing afternoon to cross the road and walk back into the swarming station. Picking up an Evening Standard she made her way to platform seventeen.

It was twelve o'clock. Downstairs Jonny and Rob were installing the wood burner. All morning they had been in and out the house. Besides Radio 1 she could hear drilling, sweeping and vacuuming and talking and sometimes laughing. Ladders leaned against the front of the house to access the chimney. Their van was on the drive, the back doors thrown open. Dust covers carpeted the hall. The chimney was swept leaving a layer of fine black dust on the thinnest lip. This, along with three months of neglect brought on a cleaning frenzy of wringing cloths and wiping.

The wood burner generated heat only dreamed of. The simplistic black stove brought the Industrial Revolution to the house. Like a brazier's furnace the glow beamed through the glass. Showers of sparks and tongues of flames licked and lapped round the logs, hissing and spluttering they broke down. Sometimes there was an echoing clomp when a log fell against the firebox. Small cracks became fissures that widened and widened in the raging heat, the charcoal disintegrating until it no longer held its shape to lightly collapse into the ash pan. Shadows danced and flickered around the room and when she carefully opened the door to 'log-on' pin-prick sparks as light as dust curled out in the draught of air. The smell of smouldering wool had her rubbing the carpet furiously, flicking the culprit back onto the hearth. Watching the fire was absorbing, tantalizing and mesmerizing. Like the sea you never tired of it. No two pieces of wood were the same, neither the air intake or the wind or the direction of the wind were the same, resulting in plaintive cries and long veils of flames that whipped round the top of the red-hot fire box and short controlled explosions and ignitions of fierce hot blasts. Her husband loved it. He loved organising the logs, selecting and even saving certain ones for their hardness or their perfumed air, bringing them in, stacking them on the slate hearth beside the red suede gauntlet. In the recess to the side of the fireplace was a cupboard and for as long as she could remember it was used as a dumping ground for magazines and clutter and a random pile of junk if there were visitors. Emptying it, she freed-up the perfect place to house the sticks, the newspapers and a plastic bucket that served as a coal scuttle.

At times the deep alluring warmth rendered her useless. It sapped her energy. With her face flushed and her body throbbing, the heat made her sluggish. Before dehydration and lethargy set in, the heat claiming her to slump in the armchair, she had to remove herself to the far end of the room or leave it altogether. With the wild unadulterated heat, she shed her indoor coat, a now shabby extra layer that went over everything else, summer and winter it was never out of reach. In its day, it had been a stylish boucle cardigan, but no longer. Apart from going to the pool, she no longer considered it acceptable to wear out. It had been bought in Monsoon in Covent Garden and she remembered that the transaction was put through the till twice and she had to contact the bank. She was fond of that look, a long lean cardigan worn with trousers and when it was new her photo was taken along with her friend at Thornbury Hall standing between the two stone lions.

It was rare that she was home alone. Not until twelve did she have the house to herself. All morning a steady stream of children had passed through, each leaving with a fruity loaf made earlier. Her husband and son were going to watch Nottingham Forest play and would not be home until seven. Firstly she fried two pieces of cod coated in seasoned flour and heated the milk for the coffee. Once she had eaten, she blitzed the hob and filled the dishwasher. Knowing there to be a message from her very modest son, she logged on. She replied and printed the multi-page attachment that had been published in the High Energy Density Physics Journal. It was such an achievement. Although she had little understanding of the content she knew that since he was four he had a tremendous capacity with numbers. Even then his headmistress used to randomly feed him lengthy multiplications or divisions and could see him working them out in his head. Behind her back she held a smiley face badge ready to stick to his green jumper. However complicated, he always got the answer. Overnight a fresh drop of Bramley apple leaves lay over the grass and under the pergola, yellow wisteria leaves lay like golden snow, they flurried and pattered to weave a mat over the slabs. Until four she was busy in the garden. She raked and swept the leaves, bagged them up and distributed them between the compost bin and the dump. Loading the car she brushed against the cotoneaster, to leave small red leaves clinging to her jumper. Mowing the grass her boots were heavy with mud. Afterwards, she went for a power walk round the block. Against the phosphorescence, the sky was sulky, the pallor of the crescent moon vague and pale behind the shrouding cloud. She came home for a much needed cup of tea and sat reading, curled on the chair by the toasty warmth of the fire.

Feeling energized from swimming she dried her hair and got herself ready. It was the last week of Phantom of the Opera and she managed to get herself a ticket for the Thursday matinee. Catching the bus allowed her the freedom of not worrying about parking and she went early in view of having some lunch, visiting the newly opened restaurant in John Lewis. Although not late it was crowded with shoppers and the queue moved frustratingly slowly. It all seemed a bit of a muddle to her but she enjoyed the interesting pasta salad and the glass of Chardonnay perched on a high stool overlooking proceedings.

Clutching their programmes the audience filed into their seats, slowly filling the auditorium. The stage was set with cobwebs and props. She sat in the stalls, almost centre stage. The mystical unfolding staging was as alluring as the music and drama. The performance was breath taking. The audience silenced, totally spellbound, enthralled and entranced by the haunting love story being played out.

Sunday 25th November. As soon as the test match from Mumbai was finished they went out for a walk. Her husband was keen to see the extent of the flooding. After days of rain, it was bright and sunny and the wind fresh. The strengthening wind had torn the remaining leaves from the trees. Dark knots of nests wedged in the branches. Barely flapping their wings, sleek black crows lifted and fell about the sky. Some walked with the gulls, foraging in the soaking wet grass. Bury Field squelched and oozed. Whole fields lay submerged, the banks breached, the river itself barely visible. Their jeans became spattered with mud. In the town they hung over the bridges looking into the murky churning water where the river should be. There was no boundary. The next day they went to Emberton to take photos of the flooding and check her husband's water level gauges concealed in the margins. The river sluiced over the rally field and into Heron Lake, the road was impassable. Looking out across the field during the night she had seen different reflections mirrored in the floodwater and knew that it had risen further. Through the leafless trees she could see from where she sat at the computer chewing on a heel of bread, that the field opposite had become a lake. Gulls spectated on the crossbars, while the ducks and swans swam between goalposts.

On Thursday the 29th of November she swam her sixth mile.

On the 30th of November she prepared the ingredients for her Christmas Cakes (stage 1). From the cupboard she took four very large mixing bowls and with surgical precision she weighed the fruit, ground almonds and spices into two and into the other two she weighed the butter and sugar. She lined the tins, one square and one round. For forty years she had made the same recipe from the same book, doubling it to make two in order to avoid the left-over fruit drying out and being wasted. She lined the tins, a painstaking but essential job to ensure that the cakes dropped out easily. The next morning (stage 2) she creamed the butter and the sugar together with the electric whisk, beat the eggs, alternately adding eggs and flour until it was smooth and light. Into each creamed bowl she tipped a bowl of fruit and combined with a large wooden spoon. Between each she dribbled the remains of the brandy and carefully spooned the mixture into the lined tins. Between stages 1 and 2 she immersed herself in a little light opera. She had been many times to the local venue but never for anything classical. At quarter to three the doors to the auditorium opened and with relief a lot of single people took their seats, thankful that the awkward feeling of waiting alone in the foyer was over. She hung her coat on the back of the tip-up-seat, no 15. A spotlight bathed The Yellow Sofa. It was a strange name for a new work, but it sat in all its glory centre stage. The strings were tuning-up, whining altogether in a flat drawn out chord. The maid appeared and bustled about busying herself and so the love story commenced. She remembered her mother speaking very highly about Glyndebourne as though it was high-brow and intellectual, on a par with the Bolshoi Ballet. Even the way she said Glyndebourne in her Scottish accent elevated its status still further so when she read the programme for the coming month in the local paper her eye was drawn and it started at 3pm.

9

Saturday 1st December. After days of pouring rain it turned cold. In the low morning sun, pink gulls lifted onto the page of blue sky. Her warm breath turned to mist in the freezing air. The brightness and the cold meant that she was continually blotting her nose and dabbing her eyes. Underfoot each blade of grass was encrusted in hoarfrost. It was like walking on muddy meringue, although firmed-up there was still some give, like semi-frozen ice-cream ready to be whipped again. Ribbons of ice had formed in the shallow puddles. They splintered and shattered as her boots pressed into them.

Sunday 2nd December. Where the sun had not struck the pavement the frost lingered, pasted to the ground in crisp bold shadows. The fat faced sheep grazed on the sunny half of their field lumbering out of her way as she crossed into Lathbury. The river had crept back to within its banks, the ground, where it had washed over the track was frozen hard. Where it had lapped and then receded, a crust of debris had formed. It was a brittle morning. Soot black, the crows drifted, their fringed feathers outstretched in the steel cold sky and a squall of pigeons rose from their feast of sprouting oil seed rape. Birds moved through the leafless trees. Stepping aside to avoid the deep puddled rut, she inadvertently caught her boot in a loop of rusting barbed wire. Suddenly the ground rushed towards her as she fell, her wrists and arms taking the brunt. As quick as she went down she was up again, patting herself down. Playing the voice recorder later did not make for easy listening. The sun was warm and although tempted she did not remove her hat. Her pace did not let-up. Turning, she faced into the sun. Sounding like an electronic synthesizer a brace of swans flew over, their zipping wings beating in perfect rhythm. On her left, a great grey field of ploughed earth, on her right cars screamed passed on the other side of the brown leafless hedge. Then, walking lightly through the farmyard she made her way towards the low lying meadows, hoping that they were not still underwater. Instead she found herself carefully picking her way between the frozen surface water. Returning via the High Street she slipped off her glove and threaded her fingers loosely through the spindles of the town's Christmas tree. Deeply, she breathed the intoxicating smell of expectation.

The rain muttered on the metal roof of the bus shelter. The cars hissed passed, their lights on. The relief of seeing the bus turning right far outweighed the uncertain duration of the wait. The bus was warm, the windows steamy and mainly full of students going to college, of blossoming girls, Lycra stretched to its limit over ample thighs, the boys, still children, wet-behind-the-ears, put together in the mornings by their mothers who only wanted the best for their sons.

Taking the bus was easy. The bother of waiting for one was far outweighed by the fact that being transported allowed her to daydream if she wanted and off-loaded the responsibility and the decision making, there was no need for a seat belt and no need to look left or right, or break or change gear and if anything happened, it was beyond her control. Instead of looking out at the rainy landscape, she briefly read the Metro on the seat. Before meeting her son at one, her plan was to start her Christmas shopping. Stepping out into the drizzle she made her way to Heals. Her theme and she usually had one, was to buy a Christmas decoration for each person. Feeling pleased, by eleven she crossed the road and slipped into the underground. Before crossing to John Lewis in Oxford Street she ran her hand fondly over the basic cardigans in Benetton and searched out the orangey coloured cardigan in Monsoon. There was a small pile of three above the orange co-ordinates. Lifting one down, she held it against her, refolded it and put it back. Breezing out of the shop she went into John Lewis and up in the lift to the third floor, hoping to buy a grey willow log basket. Seeing one on display from the opening doors she went straight to it. Her hopes were dashed. One of the handles had pulled out. And just to make sure that there were none to be had she went to the Sloane Street branch. There were none. Keeping an eye on the time she caught the tube to South Kensington and walked to Blackett Laboratory to meet her son. They ordered warm cider from the bar and went on to choose from the menu. Conversation flowed and then she mentioned the appointment. His face dissolved when she told him about the cancer. He stopped eating and turned away. His eyes filled with tears. Squeezing his arm she implored him not to worry and that she wasn't worrying and that it would be fine. There was no easy way to tell her wonderful sons but at the same time, they had to know. She distracted him with talk of shopping and Christmas arrangements. Lunch time ended and they hugged goodbye. For her he put on a brave face, but as she turned to leave, a troubled shadow fell over him. Having over an hour left before catching the train, she went back for the orangey cardigan and bought a book for her husband. Before she knew it, she was back in the kitchen preparing the dinner.

The ladder had taken up position on the landing. With the wallpapering complete and the fire installed the next task was to insulate the loft. Her husband positioned the ladder and with a great heave, launched himself into the loft to cut and lay the fourteen rolls of insulation standing to attention along the rafters. Painstakingly he had been working his way through the roof on his hands and knees but had come to a stop. He needed her help to clear some rubbish. Through the hatch he passed her a toilet cistern, various cardboard boxes filled with polystyrene, a bag of bags, a bag of coat hangers, a kite and sections of the cot. Everything was black with filth that had skittered under the tiles in the wind. The cot looked sorrowful. Pausing, she took her fingers lightly over the marks where her babies' gummy mouths had gnawed at the wood and removed the paint. For a moment she was pensive, caught off-guard, remembering their little faces, their soft peachy skin, their downy hair, the hold that they had over her. With their mannerisms not established their baby years blended together. It was hard to separate one from another. Filled with a quiet sadness she pictured herself standing over the cot watching the rise and fall of their breathing or pulling themselves up and standing at the bars waiting for her to lift them out or testing their agility, levering their arms with all their strength and stretching a leg to its limit until they were up and over and out. She pictured them upset, with tear filled eyes, sitting forlornly in their nappies when it was irritably hot and getting frustrated trying to move about in a cumbersome sleep-suit when it was cold. She saw the soft toys discarded on the floor. On her hands and knees she carefully went through the collapsing boxes of keepsakes and fading memories that her husband passed down to her, reminders of people and places, cards and calendars, old discoloured newspapers, the same headlines. Loading the car she went to the dump.

Taking herself to level 4 again she took a seat. This time it was real. This time she was there to have the now known cancerous cells removed. The Doctor explained the consent form in front of her and at the end there was a dotted line for her to sign and print her name. She lay down and was covered in a disposable sheet into which he cut a window. When the numbness of the local anaesthetic had kicked in the Dr took his scalpel and carved into her neck in order to exhume the knotty growth of fibrous tissue buried between the muscles, the tendons and the ligaments, not forgetting the membrane of veins. All the way through the procedure they talked about food and India and kitchens and their children. She could see by his hand movement that he was sewing her back together again, just lengthening the cut slightly to improve the finish. Curious to see what had been removed, he showed her the little jar. Compared with what had been the tip-of-the-iceberg visible on the surface, no more than a risen scratch that had refused to heal it looked for all-the-world like a preserved Jerusalem artichoke.

Not familiar with the all-singing all-dancing patient self-check-in system recently installed she checked herself in. It was just as easy she thought to give her name to the receptionist standing three feet from the screen. Taking a seat, she faced the Christmas tree heady with red baubles and garlands of red beading. Clear fairy lights sparked on and off. A poorly baby, red-eyed and snuffling, lay in the crux of his father's elbow. The removal of the stitches was not pleasant. There were many and feeling each tug she was glad that she had requested to lie down. Another appointment was made to check the wound.

Sandwiched between the surgery and the removal of the stitches was Christmas. Since September the pressure had been intense. For her Christmas was overrated. She battled constantly against being swept along in the relentless tide of commercialism and consumerism.

With Christmas shopping sorted she arranged the painted hazel whips and glittering twigs in a large stone jar. As each card arrived she perched it on a sill and hung minimalistic decorations from the window catches. Miniature conifers were potted-up in terracotta flower pots. Swallowed up with preparation, her energies were ploughed into cooking. Lists were revised and revised on folded A4 paper. Her last shopping expedition but one was the biggest ever in monetary terms. Her trolley was piled high with the little 'essentials' to meet her needs and apart from the artichokes everything on the list and more had been bought and eventually ferretted away in a second freezer, borrowed on a short term loan, the fridge and the cupboards. While they would not admit it, her children's expectations of her were also high. Books, magazines, recipe pull-outs and printed sheets lay spread-open in a pile on the dresser. Years ago she had moved away from the 'traditional' meal and this year it was to be a farmyard theme, a range of roasts rubbed and marinated, zinging with flavour. In the run-up, desserts were made and frozen in advance. The cake tins groaned with favourites and were labelled with a festive card. She trialled a new ice cream pudding made with advocaat and cream and bought a spring form tin in which to make it. The recipes were indulgent, subtle, laced with love and alcohol.

Nothing was spared. She cooked with butter and lashings of cream.

As a child it only appeared at Christmas time, albeit copious amounts of it, thickly applied to a trifle haemorrhaging with sherry. But as long as she could remember she had bought half a pint pot of double cream every week, delving to the back of the chiller in the supermarket to retrieve the freshest available and even though not required she would make an un-needed pudding that for health reasons, neither she or her husband should consume. It was rarely wasted. As it neared its 'use-by' date it was used up in quiches, soups, muffins, scones or simply to float in cups of coffee. Even now her children made her smile when they demonstrated her unscientific way to test for freshness. Unless there were visitors when it would be decanted into a jug and it wouldn't be 'old' cream anyway, the cream was served directly from its blue and white plastic pot, suspicion about the freshness immediately rose if it was transferred to a jug, implying that there was something to hide. Removing the clear clip-on lid, she would carefully prise off the tamper proof seal enough to let the cream pour and dipping the blade of a knife or a teaspoon into the cream she would taste it, deliberately moving it between her tongue, her lips and the roof of her mouth. If it was fresh, she swallowed with satisfaction but if it had passed its best, she collected enough saliva in her mouth and spat the whole lot down the drain then shuddered.

Even though there was a product called whipping cream, she didn't use it, preferring double, always double. Of course there was a risk of quickly over-whisking that was not so likely with whipping, but it didn't have the substance. Being well practiced, she confidently whisked on number three, knowing that a turn of a beater too many could render it looking like curds and whey, so as she neared that critical moment she reduced the speed.

She loved cream. She loved how it slipped from the pot, clinging and coating. Too heavy to splash and too thick to drip, the milky white emulsion was velvety smooth, silky rich and desirably pure. Being hugely high in fat however was not in its favour, it was the word cholesterol that spoilt her love affair with the dreamy cool indulgence, feeling a pang of guilt even if she licked the spoon or scraped the bowl with a spatula. The alternatives available were not for her, anything synthetic, 'with added sugar' or squirted from an aerosol, none met her expectations.

As young as four she could remember being thrashed for going from house to house along the terrace where they lived and breaking the foil lid on the thick glass milk bottles to filter off the cream with her fingers. It was before milk was homogenized, when the cream used to float on top of the skim, before the days of cartons and plastic containers, before fridges, not as far back as churns and jugs delivered on a horse drawn cart, just slightly more recent. Until she was caught red-handed, people up and down the lane had put it down to the blue tits.

In the winter the milk would freeze and lever up the foil lid and it would perch like a hat on top of the cream. In the summer however, before reaching the cornflakes it would be rancid from sitting on the step since sunrise and her mother lamenting over the waste. She remembered the crates of third pint bottles left stacked in the playground at school. In the winter months they were quickly emptied but in the summer the milk was sour and left with a white waxy straw poking through the silver foil lid.

For each of her children she fiddled and faffed to make them a mini Christmas cake liberally embraced with marzipan and chocolate and decorated with the colourful spots and ribbons. Nothing was too much trouble.

Thursday 13th December. In the grip of winter the air hummed in the ringing cold. The skeletal trees were clad white, each branch, each twig etched and spiked and fizzed with frost. Like a crystalized frothing mist the trees glistened and glittered silver and gold in the still, freezing air. In contrast the river brooded, turning in slow eddies. A wren made a dash to the other side. A heron stood in the classic pose used in bird books, hunched and shrugged on one orange leg amongst the frozen reeds. Perched high and stark against the barbed glass trees the crows yearned mournfully.

On Friday the 14th of December she swam her 7th mile

It was the last walk for a while. It began to rain again. It was incessant. The river rose and spread out like an inland sea. Little waves kicked-up across the field. Roads became flooded and impassable. Unable to see one of her friends at the pre-Christmas breakfast, she waded ankle deep through the flood water to give her a hug. Back home again she set the table. It was a ritual and always done well before time, arranging the four miniature conifers sprinkled with glitter, table mats, tea-lights in each place, napkins folded, cutlery laid, candles, gathering the chairs together from the four corners of the house and once complete, perusing the table to make sure that nothing had been overlooked. She hovered over the pans, lifting lids, stirring and checking. At last she felt ready for the big event. That was until she answered the phone. The call dramatically changed her spirits. It seemed that the days ahead, in an excited child-like way, the expectation that she had so eagerly awaited, simply drained away to become nothing more than a passing dream. It threw her completely, sending her careering and spiralling off course. Withdrawing, she quietly festered until the challenge had passed hoping that her act, her light busy manner, seeing to everyone's needs would disguise her harboured feelings. There was no lingering at the table, no coffee gathering momentum in the percolator, no reading the menu as the chocolates were passed around, no pouring of port into the myriad of tiny glasses along with morsels of cheese. She wondered, although it was never spoken about again, if her children realized how deflated she felt on Christmas Eve. The Christmas morning breakfast was a muddle too, the table un-laid, the TV brightening up the corner. Like the previous evening, it was not prolonged, no cups refilled. Her husband was hostile, slipping to mute unless targeted for a reaction. Not until the safety of the Boxing Day sport did he loosen up.

Returning for the wound check at the end of the week she sat facing the window in which she could see the reflection of the Christmas tree lights flashing on and off. Somehow all the festivities seemed superfluous.

People would say that she was over sensitive. She couldn't help that, she cared passionately about food, what she was serving and how she served it. It went way beyond nourishment and calorific values. She saw it as fundamental, at the heart, the very essence of her family, a way of devoting herself to them in a maternal, nurturing way. It was about her hands, preparing, cutting and slicing, whisking and kneading and having the knowledge and understanding to do these operations, either by using her initiative or by following a recipe. She liked to strike a chord with their senses. There was nothing worse than food that tasted of nothing, bland, like cardboard models resembling food. And most important of all, there had to be a generous helping of love. It didn't matter if it was a posh meal or a passing snack; to her it was intensely personal and had to be right, anything less met with her disappointment.

Sunday 30th December. Within moments of leaving the house, the hem of her jeans had escaped from a sock leaving a gaping funnel for the cold air to circulate. She stopped to undo the lace of her boot and re-pleat it firmly back in position. After days of dreary rainy weather it was dazzlingly bright. The wind was cool. The low winter sun filtered through the thin high branches of the leafless trees. Although seldom free from the noise of the surprisingly busy Sunday morning traffic, she could hear her earrings gently tinkling and the birds twittering and tweeting, laughing and singing. She nodded and said good morning to the passers-by. One lady on her mobility scooter walked her two dogs, Pekingese dogs sporting great ruffs of fluff round their comical faces. Further on there were runners their gluteus taut, outlined in Lycra and cyclists, stealthy, finely tuned and powering along. North Lake was brimming and lapped over the grass. She had never seen it so full. Two wavy bands of debris left as the water receded showed where it had been even higher. The lake sparkled and shone like a silver coin. Around the edges dead reeds leaned in the wind. Where the wind and lashing rain had strewn and deposited great banks of weed across the path it smelt faintly of sea weed and as the water had drained away it left in its wake, nests of matted green netty tulle littered with feathers, plastic bottles, plastic lids, lighters, cans, bits of plastic and bits of paper. Too wet to scamper, the thick brown slurry of sodden leaves glued themselves to the ground in a pulpy soup. Light smoky clouds brushed through, the wind ruffling the great expanse of the South Lake, armadas of honking geese took to the waves. Lapwings stood neatly on the wooden jetties sunning themselves. By eleven people were out and about airing their children, some trying to stay calm when their complaining child refused to comply and others smug, glad that it was not them. Out of the wind she could feel the sun on her back, she removed her hat.

10

Taking up where they had left off before Christmas they walked and talked, glad to be out of the house away from the kitchen sink and family demands. Although she knew where she was, it left her feeling like a tourist in an unfamiliar place. In the last thirty five years the new town had crept and curled round the fragmented hamlets and villages, hiding from view the once great houses, rectories, manors and picturesque cottages with their sash windows, their sweeping drives and their fine front doors. They had been crowded out with new-builds. The new grid system had avoided them and for her they had become forgotten. They wove through the intricate network of footpaths that joined them together, taking them over the A5 and the railway and up towards the Hub, the latest living/office/ eatery development on wide empty pavements. Pushing open the heavy glass door they took a table in the window, overlooking nothing more than a draughty walkway. Removing their coats and scarves they hung them over the backs of their chairs. The waitress pestered. It was rare that they hurried. They waved her away, they had barely sat down and weren't ready to order anything. Once settled they perused the menu, then promptly dissolved into conversation again. The waitress returned. Again she slipped the notebook back in her pocket. It wasn't as though the restaurant was busy. Eventually they ordered a bottle of Pinot Grigio, a jug of water and their meals from the set menu. It was a start. She ate olives in profusion, cured ham, mussels and crème brulee. From there, they crossed the Piazza to the bar round the corner. Pulling up by the fire with a bottle of red, they sat not wanting the day to end. Wishing each other a Happy New Year they went their separate ways.

The women came in in dribs and drabs glad to be in out of the cold damp evening. They chatted and said hello as they removed their coats and took their seats around the room. The hand bell on the table was rung. Obediently they stood up, including her, and sang Jerusalem. The meeting started with the minutes of the last meeting followed by much shuffling of paperwork, a list of events for the coming year was relayed and menus for the forthcoming meal read out. Then she was introduced. Arriving early, she had organised the small round table allocated to her with her precious notebooks and books which she displayed on a small book shelf. For eight months she had known about the talk. It had been her intention to give talks to local groups about her writing but at the same time was loathed to commit herself. Over and over she had composed what she wanted to say and as advised she should have made use of her voice recorder. Instead, she drafted and re-drafted, fine-tuning her talk and selected readings from her books, timing herself to an hour. It was a long time to speak and hold the ladies attention. And so she devised a little activity for them, duly handing cards and pens round she asked them to brainstorm something that they might iron. She had written about ironing before. In her opinion it was an underestimated skill. She shared her example. "I could have said, I ironed the shirt, instead I wrote."

Taking the rattling ironing board from the airing cupboard in the dining room, I know it's a strange place for an airing cupboard, but it had once been the kitchen, she set it up in the kitchen where there was more room and depending on the time of day it was, she could look out over the garden or listen to the radio. There was room for the different piles of ironing. From the broom cupboard she removed the iron from its rack inside the door, stood it on the ironing board, plugged it in and switched it on. Shaking the brushed cotton shirt pulled from the laundry basket she unbuttoned where in his haste her husband had pulled it off over his head. In the background the iconic signature tune of Last of the Summer Wine played. She could hear the audience laugh. She ironed without thinking, instinctively, in a no-nonsense fashion, in other words, she just got on with it. She ironed the collar on the wrong side first; it was well worn and fraying badly from rubbing against her husband's neck. A fit of turning collars had rendered otherwise good shirts wearable again. In five months her husband had failed to notice this exacting skill. Turning it over, she ironed the right side of the collar, the old underside. Then she laid the left sleeve on the board and ironed the cuff and the sleeve on one side then the other, standing the iron on its heel each time she manoeuvred the shirt. Then she laid the right sleeve on the board and repeated the process. All the time little puffs of steam spluttered from the sole plate followed by much hissing when she stood the iron up. Hoisting the shoulders of the shirt over the end of the ironing board, smoothing and easing the fabric with her fingers she ironed from the placket on the buttonhole side towards the buttons. The ironing board squeaked like an old bedstead. From there it was straightforward, mainly flat fabric, taking the point of the iron into the box pleat on the back yoke, over the French-flat seams and the lumpy spare buttons attached to the label. Lifting the shirt by its collar, she folded it at its shoulders, enclosing the sleeves and folding it in half. Upstairs she draped and buttoned it around a wire hanger and hung it along with the others in the wardrobe.

She encouraged the women to make use of all the 'Ws' when?-why?-where?-who?-what?

They were keen to share their ideas. One lady wearing red sitting to her right, talked about her white damask table cloth and that she ironed it in exactly the same way as she had been taught at school in her domestic science lessons and that in turn reminded her of doing envelope corners for her bed-making badge in Guides, which she still does now. Another told the group about ironing her husband's seersucker pyjamas so that they felt nice to put on. Before the much needed tea there were endless raffle numbers to be drawn and prizes presented, it seemed that everyone won something. And then there was the competition which she was asked to judge. Items beginning with 'N' had been exhibited and she had to choose a first, second and third. She insisted that she gave her reasons for the napkin and napkin ring being first, the narcissi bulbs being second and the needle box being third. It was explained that each person accrued points and these were logged on a spread sheet and totalled at the end of the year when a trophy for the most was presented. Collecting her things together she finished her tea, put on her coat and stepped out into the drizzle. In the glossy magazine delivered at the end of the month to more than 21 thousand homes was a photo of the evening and a write-up from the W.I. branch secretary.

Wednesday 9th January. Being lunch time people were out and about. Some were having a cigarette, the smell carried on the air. On leaving the house there had been a programme about local authorities investing their pension funds in the tobacco industry.

Twenty minutes from leaving the house on a glorious winter afternoon she entered Bury Field via Mill Street, a desirable road of Victorian terraced houses, with barely room to swing a cat and certainly not to park the car. A dog barked ferociously at the Mill House stable yard, she could hear hooves on the concrete and the dog reprimanded. Rain during the night had rendered the ground once more to a squelching bog. Water lay, truly saturated, walking on slightly higher ground made no difference. Squelch, squelch, squelch. Jeering crows scraped, tearing the muffled silence. Further round the field, armed with all their paraphernalia, the model aeroplane enthusiasts were making their way to their spot on the rise and at the stables that ran the length of the hedge, she could hear the horses being walked about. In the quietness of the narrow track, away from wide open field blackbirds, robins, blue-tits and a wren rustled through the scaffold of hedge, preoccupied with hopping about and scooping along, toing and froing, calling and singing, enjoying the pale shafts of sunlight that filtered through.

The track had got wider and wider as people searched for a cleaner footing. Through the trees she could see the traffic on

Wednesday 9th January.

the motorway. Disturbing a gaggle of geese ahead, the great commotion took-off in front of her. Bare youthful willows cast shadows in the glass-calm lakes, where moorhens ran across the water and the wakes from the duck convoys broke the surface. An hour later she was crossing the river and instead of walking up towards the farm she turned right then left over a weathered stile and followed the footprints across the field. Clearly she was going to miss a corner of the circular walk but could see that the route would bring her through a different farm and back to the familiar path. In the far distance the arms of the wind turbines were still. Where the river had flooded into the field, the ground was soft and thick with mud. Her boots became heavier and heavier. Not until the track was more elevated was it less muddy. As though it knew it was displaced, the lying surface water quivered and everywhere anxious dribbles of muddy water leaked and seeped, rinsing slowly back towards the river. Without a care the sheep shuffled and nudged at the grass. Passing through the High Street she stopped at the Co-op for bread and milk.

Even if it was dark, she threw up the blind. Swinging into the rhythm of the day she filled the kettle and flicked the switch. Moving to the dresser she turned on the radio. While all this was going on she started to empty the dishwasher, pulling the bottom basket forward first, decanting the cutlery to the right drawers and all the pots and pans to the tea-towel spread out on the table. Pulling out the upper basket she also dispatched the mugs and glasses to the tea towel to avoid white watermarks spoiling the surfaces. Darting here and there she put it all away and folded the tea towel. Having the company of the radio quietly murmuring in the background was part of her routine in the morning. It was not so much listening to the importance and seriousness of the world news, wars, business or current affairs interspersed with regular time checks, but the reassurance that the broadcasters imbued. Their integrity convinced. The Anchormen (men as in men and women) used their three hours of air time in an engaging way and while most of the time they remained neutral and professional, there were hints of argumentative frustration when they were drawn into heated debate with an interviewee, rattled, afraid to say something that might jeopardise the programme or they might otherwise regret, but even fallible at times for the occasional faux pas. She didn't like the presenters butting in and taking over, nor did she expect poor language or grammatical errors. 'There is some challenging questions'. Between items they bantered between themselves and tossed dry cynical comment to the listener. Into the last hour they started to relax and as the hands neared nine o'clock, she imagined them sitting back in their swivel chairs and stretching, the men would reach for their ties and loosen them, the women would reach down to their cavernous bags slumped on the floor and rummage for their phones, there was a flippant almost joyous edge as the programme wound-down for the morning.

It had been over three weeks since she had shopped. It wasn't so much that she needed food, because apart from milk and bread, there was plenty to last another week. Instead, she needed other things like a new kettle, ink for the printer, another bucket and long matches, things that she grudged buying, especially the ink. Also, the lying snow bothered her.

Saturday 12th January. To avoid her husband's running commentary on the match that was about to start she wrapped-up, pulled down her hat and went out in the biting cold. For an hour and a half she powered along. Into the field, up and over to the far corner, her elongated shadow fell pale across the grass. Underfoot was very slightly firmer, ice had started to form. Leaving the field at the Mill House, a delivery van was backing up along the street, an exacting skill in such a narrow road, its reversing alarm bleeping insistently. Crossing the road she followed the river through the church yard. While some ducks dabbled, taking shelter along the edges others fluffed themselves up against the intense cold, resigned. Braced they lined up in twos and threes on the grey silt bank, their heads tucked in, biding their time. Continuing her walk, she turned left passed the glitzy Aston Martin's showroom, opposite the artist's impression of the pending Tesco store and on to the cemetery where on passing she read the inscriptions on the headstones, and then through the gate across the swimming pool car park to join the River Ouzel. The banks were barren. In places miserable brown reeds lay dead and rotting along the margins. Returning home at two she was as warm as toast.

The need for a new swimsuit took her off to the shops. Her present one had faded to the point of looking insipid and it had lost its elasticity, rendering excess limp folds of fabric. There was one and she bought it, glad to be leaving the clamouring malls of shoppers quicker than expected. Arriving home again she changed her shoes for her boots on the mat at the front door and called goodbye.

On Monday the 14th of January she swam her 8th mile. She had not been since before Christmas, partly because of the maintenance closure and partly because of not wanting to submerge her wound. The persistent flurries of snow did not put her off. She wore her new costume, glad to feel contained once again in the grip of Lycra. As always it was busy, the usual faces still bobbing along the slow lane.

Tuesday 15th January. She scoured along the frosty ground where only the other day it had been steeped in water. A crust of ice had formed in the wide shallow puddles and she remembered her children one Sunday morning, red-faced and breathless with exertion, skating, slipping over and laughing. She had taken photos. There was one amongst the applique of photographs sandwiched behind glass in the hall of them holding hands, bobble-hatted and young.

Where it remained boggy she sloshed from tussock to tussock. On leaving the field at Mill Street, a couple, older than her, were approaching the kissing gate. Within seconds the woman passed through and turned as though dancing to kiss her partner on the mouth before he joined her for their walk. A small, bored, home-alone dog yapped for attention as she walked along Mill Street. Calling in at the library she claimed a new title from the swivelling paperback shelves.

Wednesday 16th January. A ghostly pall of freezing fog took hold. Nothing escaped the plunging temperatures and penetrating cold, the needle sharp wrath of winter. The muffled air hovered. Once again trees and hedgerows foamed with hoarfrost. White lacy webs strung out between the frozen twigs. Every blade of grass was encrusted and crunched like sugar lumps beneath each step. With dependable regularity her front door key in her pocket clinked against her thigh as she trudged along, breaking the stillness, her arms swinging loosely at her side.

On Wednesday the 16th of January she swam her 9th mile.
On Friday the 18th of January she swam her 10th mile

Sunday 20th January. As forecast, snow fell again. Shadowy ledges of snow piled against the windows. The gritty granules lay surprisingly quickly over the partial thaw. Despite the numbing depth of cold she went out. Familiarity looked desolate. Parked cars in the side roads were blanketed and stippled, icicles dripped from their bumpers. Unlike her usual stride she took small measured steps. Footprints had destroyed the powdery surface, concentrating she didn't take her eyes from the compacted praline underfoot. The snow squeaked as her boots bit into the newly fallen snow. All of a sudden when her footing slipped her arms flew out and her body gasped with fear and a sudden burst of sweat. Narrowing her eyes she grazed over Bury Field. It was remote. Snow fell on snow, blowing obliquely from the side, tinkling onto her big umbrella. Smudged in the snowy distance were people walking their dogs and children sledging, laughing, and shrieking excitedly when they fell off in a heap. Hours of snow filled the heavy gunmetal sky. A haunting light fell over the white wasteland. Returning home the rugby was on the TV, in the scrum the players steamed like cattle.

Tuesday 22nd January. A lady with her dog entered the field just ahead of her. For a while, until she went off to the left, she could hear the zip of her over-trousers as her thighs brushed. It was a bleak God-forsaken view. A wreath of freezing fog had closed in blurring the hostile empty waste that stretched before her. In the eerie half-light it looked like a Dickensian marshland or a Bronte moor.

There were casualties. The day before most schools had closed. On her way to swimming she encountered a Monday morning drift of soap powder left lingering when a boy walked passed with his small clean dog. People died and crashed their cars; people fell and broke their bones. She swept round the field. Paws and claws and human prints were pressed into the snowy crust. Her small steps quickened and at times she found it difficult to stop and like a runaway car on a steep hill seeking an escape, she scanned for a foothold of virgin snow. Dying blades of grass jabbed through the icy white veneer. Big fat tears from her right eye rolled over her downy cheek to splash on her sleeve. Besides dabbing her eyes, her nose needed constant attention, continually reaching for the wodges of shredded tissues lurking in each pocket. Approaching the High Street the buildings were murky and vague. She crossed at Market Hill where once there had been a weekly market, traders selling corn and lace and animals. Although there were gaps, many of the original buildings were spared the 1960's modernization and still lined the wide high street. Needing butter she stopped off at the Co-op.

On Wednesday 23rd January she swam her 11th mile.

Dumping the three jute bags on the kitchen floor, she decanted the shopping to all the right places. While doing so her husband put it to her that he would like to go to Norfolk, a nostalgic trip to Potter Heigham, a river fronted house and a dinghy, as seen in the brochure that had come in the post earlier that morning. Simultaneously he perused the brochure and the Australian calendar removed from its place on the wall. There and then the date was fixed. Just as soon as the shopping was away she phoned and booked, filled in the details on the booking form on the back of the brochure, cut along the dotted line and put it, along with the deposit in an envelope. Finding an un-franked stamp, she carefully prized it off the envelope and stuck it to hers. Slipping and sliding on the frozen pavements they went into town to post the letter.

Glad to be on board she took a seat by the window facing the wrong way. Slightly lifting herself from her seat she looked for another, facing the right way. Resigned, she took a moment to settle. In the inviting warmth she unbuttoned her coat. It was at last a sun-bathed morning and she looked out over the glittering pink fields laid out neatly between dark fringes of hedge. Off-white sheep snuffled for grass in the snow. Nearing London the snow had all but gone but the forecasters had predicted another band before the big thaw expected later in the day and she had cleaned her boots in readiness. She had expected travelling chaos and went prepared, not planning to do more than meet up with her dear son, take in his exhibition and have some breakfast. The chaos had not materialized.

A great surge of people spewed from the train, streaming towards the delta of the city. As always the station was busy. After phoning her son she headed for the underground across the concourse. Announcements on the public address system warned of a dam, that the Northern Line was closed for pre-planned engineering work. Instead she took the Victoria Line. Like a human water course, people fed in from the tributaries, emptying and filling, dissolving away only to bubble up again, cascading down and down again on finely tuned falls where the route divided, northbound and southbound. She didn't sit. At Oxford Circus she burrowed deep underground again to the Central line, westbound or eastbound. Spilling out at Bethnal Green, she waited for her son at the entrance to the station. All the time there was a steady sunlit stream of people passing-by, some stopping to cross the road at the traffic lights or descend into the station. It was cold standing on the corner and she pulled on her furry hat. Taking in the vicinity she thought, God, Tower Hamlets is a poor borough. 1960s concrete blocks must have been forward thinking at the time, but how tired and desperate they looked on that late January day, there were no leaves on the trees to soften the harsh reality of the social deprivation. In the shadows of the looming tombs, the dilapidation of the crumbling turn of the last century housing, given over to shops, shuttered and barricaded, daubed with graffiti, strewn with rubbish. It was sorrowful. She met her son as arranged and together they walked along the shiny, rain-washed pavements to The Gallery Café, into the arms of a good breakfast of porridge laced with almonds and banana even though she had asked for plain, soda bread and mushrooms and coffee. Her son's framed art work adorned the walls, expertly hung, adding a comfortable ambiance to the thriving retro café. Her son had let her decide where they sat and she had stood for a moment, briefly looking around, not especially for a table, but at the light airy room, the whitewashed walls, windows at each end, the trestle tables flung with printed plastic coated cloths, the jam jars of flowers arranged on each, the mishmash of chairs and the counter with its pastries and gaudy cup-cakes. Removing their coats they sat below the iconic picture titled *Untitled (Light)*.

It seemed strange sitting in the café, nobody knowing how special each piece of work was to her son. And him, the artist sitting there, knowing everything there was to know about them and the customers apart from her, knowing nothing. How proud he was to show her his work. How proud she was of him, privileged to recognize his achievement, commitment and dedication to his art, striving to perfect, overcoming long days of nothingness in the company of dreams, when no ideas will come. It would be interesting to see how many people would move away from their comfort zone to read the labels carefully placed beside each picture. She doubted that there would be many.

Lingering, they took photos and made their way towards Columbia Road where they dipped in and out of the shops and Arnold Circus where they stood looking over the tree-lined streets fanning out from the circus, the handful of up-market shops selling rustic loaves hand-crafted by artisans and earthy organic vegetables, the air filled with raucous crows gathering in the branches and duly she ticked them off her things-to-do-list. Her son, knowing the area well took her to a gallery in an up-coming road off Shoreditch High Street and nearby where graffiti was making its mark then into The Owl and the Pussycat for a drink. "When I grow rich say the bells of Shoreditch." They hugged and said goodbye at Highbury and Islington station. By four the sun hung low, lighting up the view from the train, the trees stark against the melting backdrop. The next day, the rising water dislodged the snowmen standing between the goalposts and carried them downstream like icebergs. Like fragile butterfly wings, the pansies fluffed themselves up and from the kitchen window she could see the snowdrops nestling beneath the apple tree.

11

Forty years is a long time. It should be marked in some way. She doubted that her husband was going to surprise her by whisking her away to some far flung island, so she set to, organizing a special lunch for the special day. She would have the table in a square shape. She drew up a menu of punchy flavours then taking a piece of A4 paper wrote a very long shopping list.

It was the 1st February. All day her husband had been busy clearing and sorting out a border where the trellis had fallen into disrepair. This justified going to the Rose and Crown for a drink.

At the beginning of February she went to her local travel agents. For a long time, well since they went to Melbourne eight years ago she wanted to do the test series in Australia, only doable once retired and the time had come. She presented the dates to Penny and left her to see if she could tailor the trip to suit her needs. Just over a week later she went in to check the progress. There were flights and hotels neatly matching the dates all printed out on several sheets of paper. With a little adjustment by the following week the trip was booked.

Monday 4th February. The sky was plain blue and went on for ever. It was too good not to be out breathing the cold sharp air. The sun more than compensated for fierce biting wind. Although the flooding from the sudden thaw had subsided it was still wet. Prints of bikes and boots and hooves and paws had pressed into the fudgy mud and negotiating where to place her feet slowed her up as did the weight of it adhering to her boots. Sinking ankle deep at times she muttered ugh and oh in disgust. In her head she could hear her mother complaining. The treetops roared and pitched like the sea, the bark chafed with the relentless friction. Small branches and twigs were snapped and strewn. The wind shifted through the empty hedgerows. Just ahead of her, a great flock of pigeons swept round the field swooping from willow to willow. Minding the water-filled ruts and the loop of rusting barbed wire that had tripped her up she made her way along the rough puddled tracks to where she turned along the hedge and down into the farmyard where the Labrador bounded up to her, barking and sniffing her gloves, the small dog following. Consoled, they left her to walk through. In the sunlight the willows took on an orangey bloom. Crows and jackdaws drifted, their mournful cries clawed at the wind.

Getting a newspaper on Saturday was becoming a habit. The first thing she did was to split it into its various sections and discard the flyers and the stuffers. It sat strewn and folded on the dresser and took all week to read, the crossword teasing and often not completed without the help of the Thesaurus. Even though the choice of viewing was rarely hers, she turned and checked the TV page each morning. High Noon was going to be on at 1pm, when she got home. It was a western she remembered seeing a long time ago in black and white, with Grace Kelly and Gary Cooper. The film, with a sense of impending doom unfolds in real time, the tension unbearable, the music tormenting. And so she sat on her own folded on the settee watching daytime TV for eighty five minutes.

Wednesday 6th February. She returned from swimming to find that the publishers had emailed her manuscript to proof read. It was exciting and it was happening. Her mind ran like the wind. She did some ironing to calm and contain herself. On the weather map it seemed that there was one big wide arrow blowing in from the Arctic covering the whole country. The wind was fierce and bitterly cold. With her fake fur hat clamped to her head, she went out for a power walk. On reaching Bury Field her duffle hood went up as well. In the numbing wind her eyes leaked uncontrollably. She squeezed them tight and the wind snatched away the water. Easily a hundred crows walked around pecking at the windswept grass. Others flew low to join them and she wondered what was so interesting to crows in that particular grass rather than anywhere else. Although she tried not to, in her head she was sounding like her mother, grumbling about the horrible squelching ground. On the way home she bought milk in the Co-op, always useful.

Friday 8th February. Knowing that she would be cooking and eating for the entire weekend she scrawled a note and left it on the table, 'Doing the Willen walk. Left at 9.30am.' wrapped-up and went out. When doing a long walk, she usually wrote the time, just in case. She often gave herself a little challenge, like not walking on cracks. On that Friday it was not to blow her nose until absolutely essential and for at least a mile she didn't, which equated to fifteen minutes. In between sniffs, her warm breath puffed-out in time with her step. There were parts of the walk where she felt just very slightly apprehensive. There were two lorries parked, one of which appeared to have problems. She could see by the number plates that they were Polish, then she heard one of the men say "Dobry dobry." There was no reason she could think of to make her feel suspicious of the two men other than the intense resentment that had built up against them since they joined the EU, filling their schools and hospital waiting rooms, as though they were entitled. A tide of rime fringed the glassy patches of polished ice and the thin sun made no impression on the freezing temperatures. Like a silver shimmer it fell over the placid lake and apart from the ducks, the swans and the geese nothing stirred. Distant trees silhouetted against the pale liquid light were still. There were people about, a runner, a gaggle of women walking, a man in a high-viz jacket picking rubbish, dog walkers and the couple in front of her. She was walking on their weak shadows and had to overtake them. As she walked on and round South Lake, the wind picked up, breaking up the surface into a jagged pattern. For some reason that she couldn't fathom, she always walked clockwise round the lakes.

As she knew she would, she spent Saturday 9th February preparing and cooking ready for Sunday. Her menu was extensive, nibbles, soup, cheese-straws and bread, Thai fishcakes, crab-cakes, chicken satay, individual quiches, chicken in white wine and soured cream, trays of roasted vegetables, wilted spinach and leeks, asparagus, chocolate roulade, vanilla cheesecake, raspberry and almond torte, cheese and biscuits, chocolates and of course champagne, wine, coffee, beer. The square shaped table was perfect. Laying the table; she loved laying the table. Cheery polyanthus took centre stage in a terracotta pot, mats and napkins and all the cutlery she possessed, candles. It was arranged for one o'clock. Between courses there were lulls when everyone drew breath. Forty years ago she had never envisaged how it would be, the rich tapestry of life, her adorable sons, her steadfast husband, loyal and dependable.

All week she had threatened to go to the pool but her body could not muster the energy or stand the cold. With the altered timetable for half term she felt encouraged. She was not graceful, but the lady insisted that she was while they stood for a moment in the warmer than average pool. The lady envied her children swimming around her like seals, longing to be able to swim like them.

Opening up her emails, there was a review from her cousin about her book Domestic Science. She didn't ever get the impression that he suffered fools gladly, nor did he wax lyrical about things, they were either black or white. It was such an unexpectedly warm compliment.

I have finished the book. I thought it would be all about cupcakes, Demerara sugar, egg whites and oven temperatures.

I was wrong. Having read it, I now see the title has a much wider interpretation.

I thought your style was jagged. By that I mean I did like the way it jumped from scenario to scenario as each paragraph was read. This kept me interested and at times I wanted to know more before the story moved on. I soon discovered, however, that several pages further on I did find out more and this kept me holding the book. Sometimes it was funny, sometimes it was sad and sometimes I detected a wee undercurrent which intrigued me and I wanted to know whether or not I was right.

It was beautifully written with nice descriptive language and this, too, kept me holding the book.

I await "Patchwork" dropping through my letter box.

The three friends boarded the bus for Cambridge at 9.30am. Expecting to pay she held her ten pound note, a purse of change and her bus-pass which had dropped through the door the week before. Imagine her delight to be told that she needn't pay anything. The morning was cold and crisp. All the way, spokes of dazzling sun flooded through the windows. Their faces squinted in the blinding light. The heating blared from beneath the seats, leaving all three of them heady and wilting from the warmth. Thick and throbbing they were glad to be off the bus and sitting outside later for their coffee they gradually shook off the wretched feeling. Restored, they took to window shopping, strolling, and having lunch and a late afternoon drink before catching the bus home again. Judy was travelling on the Norwich and after saying goodbye they walked to wait for the bus. In the time that they waited it grew dark. The file of waiting people filled the bus. On the big warm bus she felt safe and secure. Weaving through the city, lights dimpled. With blinds and curtains not yet closed, windows lit up. Like a moth, her eyes were drawn to the lights blinking on around her. Flicking from one glowing window to another she briefly intruded. From basements to attics, she saw no more than a fleeting glimpse of cornices, lights, tables being laid, bags being dumped, a wagging tail, a screen saver, a vase of flowers.

She sat again on level 4, waiting. The extractor vibrated and its draught aerated. The man to her left was restless, crossing and uncrossing his arms, shuffling his legs, in between chewing gum with jaw-aching urgency he seemed unaware of his tuneless humming. On her right, another man, much younger, played on his phone. The nurses and staff went about their day, showing people through the blue doors of the consulting rooms. The appointments were running late. Once again she was advised to avoid the sun, cover up, and wear a hat. Had she had the literature? No. The nurse shuffled the sheets together and handed them to her. At home her friends waited. It was half term and her dear friend and her husband had stayed a couple of days. As it happened both husbands were poorly and not their usual fired-up selves. They had all been out the day before for sausages from a very reputable butcher, visited the churchyard, seen the deer in Woburn and later done a treetop walk. Other than that they had nursed the fire, eaten and flopped in front of the TV. With their mini-break over, their friends left, leaving her husband with a streaming cold. Never good. For the next few days there was much sniffing and long drawn out sighing. Like her dear friend had done, she administered the Lemsips and put up with the sleepless nights. When they had gone and it was quiet she unfolded the sheets. She didn't doubt for a moment that today's appointment was the last. She had a flat red scaly mark on her shin like the one described and the information implied that it could pose a problem. She remembered her godmother flinching and wincing with pain when the nurse on her knees carefully dressed the oozing ulcers that were slowly devouring her flesh. Also, her skin was itchy at times. She wanted to rip at it with her nails.

Tuesday the 26th of February = 1 mile 12th mile.

She pulled hard on her hat. A handful of latex came away in her hand. Without the firmness of the edge, the hat was useless and she threw it in the recycling bin.

The need for a new one took her off to the shops on the bus. While there, she went into MK Gallery. The exhibition reflected a different way of looking at the everyday things around us. She liked the Dandelions, painted she thought hurriedly, directly onto great lengths of cartridge paper and fastened to the wall just as hurriedly with a dressmaker's pin in each corner. The film of the snowman learning to ski made her smile. There was an installation of night-time videos. Thrown-up onto the plain white walls were clips of urban scenes that usually go unnoticed and hurried passed. Instead of being ignored the artist brought them to attention, swirling rubbish, caught in the movement of the wind skittering paper cups scurried and scampered, a discarded can propelled around, stopped abruptly then gathered momentum again, hooded youths having a kick-about. The angry can rolled round and round in her head as she crossed the road for the bus home.

Most days she checked Amazon to see how her books ranked. After a bit of an improvement they were slipping down again. With a sudden burst of enthusiasm she emailed two daily papers and a magazine, encouraging them to check out her books. Thirsting for a reply she was hopeful, though in her heart she knew it would come to nothing. From one, an Out of Office Autoreply came back almost instantly. Having any reply was something. There were no replies. She dreamed of being believed, of her books being taken seriously. Her publisher had paid warm compliments and from people who had read them also, but she feared that without a helping-hand from the bookshops or media drawing her books to the public's attention, recognition would quickly fade. However she was not giving up or giving in. Ideas whirled in her head.

Monday 25th February. After what seemed to be days indoors, she had to be outside, however cold. Smuts of bitter rain fed in on the raw east wind. There were dog walkers and a huddle of young mums with pushchairs and maybe dogs, but she couldn't see and didn't like to look. It was bleak and lifeless and she muttered the usual disgust as she unfalteringly plunged her boots into the soupy mud. The need to be back by eleven for the blind man curtailed the length of the walk, making it all the more intense. The blind man was going to hang the blinds, not that she or her husband couldn't do the simple task, but it was part of the service. For months she had looked at blinds, nothing was quite the colour. Unlike the large superstores where anonymity was a blessing, in her local shop she was committed once over the threshold and felt compelled to buy. The lady lifted the heavy books of samples onto the counter. The very first book fell open at the fabric she in the end chose. Absently she flicked through the book before her and the lady went to great lengths to find others, folding the swatches to mark the pages. No, the first sample was the one. Within a couple of days the blind man came to measure, insisting that it was part of the service. Sensing her eyes roaming over his shoes in the hall, he stepped out of them and padded through the house in his socks. Writing the invoice took longer than measuring. A deposit was required. Turning she opened the corner cupboard door that housed her books, magazines, occasionally used jugs and numerous coffee pots. Reaching for the red enamel tea pot she emptied its treasured contents of pound and two pound coins, collected for the sole purpose of plying car park machines. The soft-close door shut behind her. The blind man looked on astonished. Well trained, the son of the blind man who came to hang the blinds a week later removed his shoes without thinking.

Tuesday 26th February. A cold thick cloak of daunting cloud persisted. Where the home-alone dogs lived a boy, about twelve approached. "Excuse me." He said. "Have you got a tissue?" Instantly she could see why he needed one. Opening her bag she quickly saw that there were none. Then, from the depths of her pocket she produced her only crumpled tissue and opened it out for him to see that although it had been used to dab her face, there was a smear of lipstick and a brush of make-up, it was still reasonably clean. Wiping the stream of dark red blood between his nose and his top lip, he was grateful and thanked her. She told him that it looked much better and he smiled. Into Bury Field the view was smudged. Trees loomed through the fret and quickly her duffle coat was speckled with damp. She felt like her mother when she blew her nose, the way she held the hanky in her claw-like grasp squeezing the red tip of her nose with her thumb and index finger, blotting to remove the drips to return her bare hand to the warmth of her glove. She had the look of her mother, chapped and pinched. She had her nose. Her mother was fond of fine lawn hankies, never without one, tucked up her sleeve or clutched in her gnarled bony hand. She boiled them in an old saucepan and ironed them whilst damp into razor-sharp creases, hanging them over the radiator in the hall to finish off. Losing one was the end of the world. She declined tissues. If she had any, given as gifts, it would be visitors to the house that made use of them.

Wednesday 27th February. The grey solemn days continued. A glimmer of sun in the afternoon persuaded her to do the circular walk. Other than the days drawing out, she hoped to see some signs of spring. And she did. In the narrow track a flourish of white starry blackthorn blossoms braved the brutal east wind. Here and there a smattering of green broke through the hedgerow. Winter had at last released its grip on the unfurling hawthorn leaves. Hazel catkins and pussy willows vied for attention. Where there were gaps between the trees a pale light fell over the dirt track, the birds bustled from branch to branch, twittering. Gathering rooks took to the tree tops. At the farm she was greeted by the dogs. The Labrador bounded along, the terrier yapping annoyingly at his heels. The Labrador sniffed at her gloves. She passed the sniff test and all went quiet. The collie was too old to care. Passing through the farmyard she could hear the animals in the sheds, bleating and mooing. Rounding the field the rasping wind caught and rustled the copper beech. Ahead, beating and flapping their ragged wings, a company of crows rose altogether to settle again some way off on the brown ploughed field. The countryside was tidy, all ready. Her right glove was continually on and off, firstly to dab her nose, secondly to retrieve the voice recorder from her bag, push the miniscule on/off button and the slightly bigger 'rec' button, and thirdly approximately half way she ate two pared and segmented mandarins. Without reading the label she could not tell a clementine from a Satsuma or a tangerine, or a mandarin. She put her lack of knowledge down to the fact that it wasn't a native fruit, unlike apples which she could identify easily. One thing for sure, they weren't 'easy peelers'. It had taken a dextrous hand wielding a serrated knife to remove the stubborn peel. She felt sure that branding fruits 'easy peelers' would only encourage people to think that there really were such fruits. The thirst quenching juice hit the mark. Finishing the segments she pulled on her glove again. Where there had been thin silver sheets of floodwater, she counted twelve swans bathing, sitting as though floating amongst the green sprouts of wheat piercing through the soil. The glimmer of sun had been short lived. Again slouching cloud stole across the sky. It was the last day of February.

12

Friday 1ˢᵗ March. It was March. Without fail the winter bond was loosening its grip and she felt as though she was emerging out of a burrow, bleary-eyed from a long hibernation. There were things to do. Looking out over the road, it was still cold and drab. Beside her, however, on the 'Scotland From The Air Calendar' dates were already earmarked. Her right hand was cold. She had wasted enough time at the computer. Sounding like electricians feeding cable through the eaves burley pigeons were in the gutter above the window where she sat scrabbling at the moss that had bobbled from the roof. Logging off, she left a note on the table; 'Having a fast walk.' Crossing the road, she thought of Alice then as she reached the gate she breathed deeply the lingering smell that she loved, the intoxicating smell of Mr Wood's pipe. "Good afternoon." He said, removing the pipe from his mouth. The wind was invigorating, as cold as ever. Not even the ducks took to the grey-green water. Following the path through the graveyard, clusters of snowdrops hugged the bank and the path was slippery in places where the river had stayed too long and the silt deposits had not dried up. She crossed into Mill Street and into Bury Field. It was very slightly drier, like Plasticine. There were a few dog walkers. Slipping through the gap, across the car-park and home, she had been an hour. Her husband had not come into the house and read the note.

It was arranged that she went to see Alice, as promised when she bumped into her when walking into town back in November. She wanted to tell her about the drift of aconites that had snuggled up through the grass by her front door. Alice had moved to North London to be near to her surviving family.

Troubled with a fall and her arthritic knees, she was no longer able to give the garden that she loved the care and attention it deserved; she finally surrendered to the move.

It was a hard-core, unforgiving morning, penetratingly cold at -4 degrees and she was wrong to think that the freezing wreath of low cloud would lift and develop into a bright spring day.

The 7.42 train was running 10 minutes, then 20minutes late. The 8.10 train was due and everyone shifted platforms only to be informed that the 7.42 would only stop at Watford and then Euston. Most passengers, including her returned to platform 2. As soon as the 8.10 train departed there was an announcement. The 7.42 train would terminate at Watford. A universal chorus of curses rang out amongst the passengers waiting. Convinced that she would not be cold she had gone meanly dressed and left her gloves in the car. By the time the 7.42 train pulled in she had stood in the numbing cold for fifty minutes. Shedding her shoes she toasted her feet on the heater to thaw-out. They finally left Watford at 9.23. The delay changed her morning. Any intention of going to St Martin's was abandoned. Instead, she headed for Tate Britain. Ahead Big Ben struck ten. The river was busy, tourist boats already on the move. With the Houses of Parliament the backdrop, the never ending tide of tourists clamoured and thronged on Westminster Bridge for the iconic photo. Re-joining the river on Millbank she walked along to Tate Britain. On her right there was a great commotion of chainsaws where a proud line of plains were being lopped and shredded. A keen wind fed off the grey ruffled tideway, joggers probably grateful for its refreshing coolness. She remembered the building from her student days, but had not been since. Taking in Frank Bowling's Poured Paintings she sat warming herself in the empty gallery, drop, roll, slide, drip. She submerged herself in Constable and Turner, the landscapes and the seascapes, the views that she knew Henry Moore's masks and Jake Chapman's Family Collection. Before leaving for Finchley, she sat and ate a banana. Finding Alice in good spirits she was immediately given a guided tour of her two bedroomed flat. It was light, airy and easy. She wanted for nothing. She didn't even long for her garden. A black and white picture of her stood on the table by the window. Taken in Cyprus in shimmering white heat, when Alice was young, her hair thick and dark. She carried a bucket bag. Her printed summer dress moved in the throbbing waft of air. She watched Alice's face cloud with memories. Probably sixty years had slipped past. She wanted to know more, but didn't like to ask.

The event at the end of March was looming. It had not been expected and frightened everyone concerned. Her son's special news back in November that he was to be a father caught her unawares. A mixture of fear and excitement and relief drained from him when he told her standing in the hall. She could tell that he was apprehensive and didn't know what to think and it was hard for her not to show mixed feelings. There was no need to speculate further. It was to be a boy.

Everything seemed suddenly uncertain. She held tightly to her friend's comment. "It will be the making of him." She didn't launch into knitting matinee jackets and bonnets as her mother had done for her forthcoming baby, him standing before her now. All she thought about was the instability, the lack of money, another mouth to feed, the pressure, making do and getting by, lurching from month to month, learning to live with his space invaded, taken over with disposable nappies and a push chair parked like a chair in the rented one-up one-down house.

Pushing the heavy curtain of winter aside, spring made an entrance. For two days there was a splash of sun, a taster no more than a ripple of spring but enough for her to launch into the garden again. Regretting now not doing it in October, she needed to prune the lavender, a painstaking job. The sun fell over the dead stems and the sprouting growth and she set too with the secateurs. It took all morning. Then she cut the lawn of moss and manicured the edges neatly. All around the air echoed with every type of mower. Over the weekend her husband had cut back the hazel for new pea sticks and the privet because it had overgrown and needed taming. A great pile of twigs and branches were heaped up for her to take to the dump. Twice she loaded the car and drove round to the dump. Once again it was the start of the relentless unstoppable growth.

For days the sky reached down and touched the earth.

Owing her son some money she needed to go to his bank. Handing the cashier his account number and the cheque she noticed her name badge. At the same time she read her son's surname, both very distinctive names. She looked at her. "You used to be my form teacher." "You had that lovely green bag." She replied. They laughed and shared a moment that seemed a lifetime away.

The assistants in the charity shop were despairing. Trade was almost non-existent. There was simply no one in the high street casually passing the time of day. She had seen the skirts weeks ago, there were several, all her size and looked as though they had been owned by the same person. She particularly liked the greenish one and there was a brown one too, identical. Popping into the cubical, she slipped off her coat and scarf. The hook had been pulled off the wall and unreasonable though it may sound, her phobia about putting anything on the upholstered button back chair wedged in the corner was very immediate and nor did she want to put her things on the floor. Gripping all her belongings below her knees she quickly pulled down her jeans and hoisted the skirts over her head and zipped them up. Really she knew they would fit.

Thursday 7th March. The dismal lifeless weather continued. Once again the field was wringing wet. On and on it rained. And it pattered steadily on the big umbrella that had a mind of its own, the loose fabric gently breathing in and out in time with her step. Skirting round the edge of the field she gave up searching out a cleaner footing and just hauled through the marshy brackish water.

They sat having a coffee where they had sat before, overlooking the butchers, watching the world go by and catching up with the news. There was a delivery. Two carcasses, a pig and a cow were being winched out of the van, suspended on meat hooks by their trotters and their shins. They hung in the passing traffic, waiting to be lifted down by the man in the bloody apron and taken inside to be butchered.

At ten she had an appointment with Lee. "When you come back, I want to be able to see that it has been cut," Her husband voiced the previous day. "A good inch." She replied when Lee asked her what she wanted cut off. "I'll lie if need be." As if there wasn't enough going on, videos played on small screens between the mirrors. 'Ain't no sunshine' came on. Although older, she remembered the song from 1973, forty years ago when she worked in a boutique. Then 'I got life' came on and she remembered Marsha Hunt singing the lyrics in the 1968 version of the musical Hair. Two other ladies were having their hair done, one sat under a drier knitting something intricate in pink. It was impossible not to overhear Lee and her talking in the salon. Arriving home, she had visitors, she could smell the toast. Remembering what she wore, the 'Hair' conversation continued. She had made a shift style dress and coat in a loosely woven furnishing fabric in shades of yellow. She remembered the yellow wet look leather sling backs with a cork heel.

It was Mothering Sunday and her children drifted in and out with cards and gifts. Despite the savage wind and the swirling snow flurries she and her son went out for a walk. Their furious pace did not let up. Having company changed the walk. They chatted all the way about this and that, the monumental skyline from the Shard, their forthcoming trip to Glasgow, people that have a bad start in life. From time to time while they walked, a stream of marathon runners filtered onto the path. Although most competitors looked like slicks of oil in their black Lycra or wore leggings and tops, some braved the weather, their bare arms chapped red-raw and blotchy with the cold. Apart from that, she barely noticed anything.

So glad to have the gel nails removed, she splayed her hands on the little brown towel. Each nail was roughed-up with an emery board. Lovingly, Eve selected a little bottle from the tray, opened it wistfully and soaked a cotton wool pad. Applying one to each nail she proceeded to wrap each in foil to keep them warm before scraping the gel off. Lovely and long-lasting as they had been her fingertips longed to be free of them. Taking up the complimentary offer, they had been applied three weeks ago. Like dark smooth liquid pools they had looked glamorous. Now, however, she no longer liked the feel where her nails had grown, leaving a distinct ridge and where on her index fingers the plastic coating had lifted and was peeling away, catching on anything. Wearing her nails longer was simply not practical. Food and earth became trapped easily and she was constantly washing her hands. She longed to cut her nails. For some jobs she wore gloves. It was never the same. Once home, she trimmed and filed her nails to a smooth almond shape. With her nails restored she launched into stripping the wallpaper in her son's room that before the extension in the 80s had been their original bedroom. She had already taped a sample of paper to the wall.

Her husband left her in the kitchen in the throes of making a pan of borsch with the last of the beetroots. She turned the radio on again. Listening to the story about Detroit she weighed out ingredients for bread, gathered the dough, kneaded the bread and put it to prove, then using the same bowl, made a batch of coconut rock buns and set the timer. With the outside temperature plunging below freezing the radiators lurched on automatically, chiming and gurgling, the water hissing and spitting through the heating system like a percussion band striking up. Upstairs she turned on the computer and while it fired up she made the bed and tidied things away. Finding hair-slides, a necklace and earrings to match her green jumper she brushed her hair thoroughly. She sat and wrote, returning to the oven when she heard the bleeper to rescue the rock buns. Outside the cloud scudded through. It was bright then dark, speckles of snow blew around. Sudden squalls brought flurries. The snarling wind howled, making its way around the side of the house and the outside toilet, jostling at the garage door and pestering the latch on the back gate. Where, over time they had lost their seals, the windows moaned and every now and then the slats on the extractor fan fluttered. Outside, the bamboo wind chime chimed impatiently under the pergola. She laid the fire.

Using up the out-of-date cream, she drank endless cups of coffee and snacked on this and that. When on her own, she had appalling eating habits. In a word, she was lazy, and that after cooking meals for over forty years felt quite entitled to be so. Unlike her neighbour who religiously cooked a meat and two veg. dinner at lunch time for herself, she did not hang about in the kitchen, preferring instead to graze on nothing in particular, cold left-overs, or a packet of ham, eaten standing with the fridge open, or grilling a whole packet of fish fingers, no vegetables, no beans, or boiling a bag of kipper fillets. If she was in town she was tempted by something ready-made, like a little pot of prawn cocktail. Straightaway she would peel off the lid take a teaspoon and stir the gloopy contents together and eat it straight from the pot standing by the sink.

Another thing she was guilty of was eating baking ingredients, tubs of glace cherries, nuts, dried fruit, marzipan and left-over squares of chocolate. This habit, this bad habit stemmed from her childhood when, seen as an extravagance and unnecessary expense, she was deprived of sweets, and to satisfy her longing she took to looking through the pantry, to discover ingredients that could be a substitute for the craving.

Her husband came home and tucked in to the inviting warm bread. Moving her chair she basked like a lizard in the fleeting squares of sun stamped on the kitchen floor, writing and reading. Looking out, she could see the smeary cloth marks on the window. The trees were a riot. Dust motes danced. At the back door her husband chopped sticks, split, sawed and stacked logs, generally keeping productively busy.

In the afternoon she wrapped-up and went out only long enough to hand deliver a letter. The scornful wind roared in the trees and pressed her jeans to her legs. The icy blasts nipped at her cheeks.

It had been five years since going to Scotland with her son. It had been their intention to turn left into Glasgow, to explore the city. But with all that scenery so close how could she turn left? Taking the 'Road to the Isle' instead, she drove straight on to Fort William stopping only at Luss for a paddle in Loch Lomond. Checking where the Gallery of Modern Art was in relation to the station and the Victorian Cemetery featured on Taggart and the nearness of the Clyde, she went to the library and picked up a book called Edinburgh and the Best of Glasgow. There was a useful map and she marked each place with a cross.

To think that it was possible to go and return in a day and spend six hours taking in the city. When it got to it, however, she thought as she often did, why am I doing this? – getting up at the crack of dawn having been awake half the night waiting for the alarm to go off. They breakfasted on bacon and egg stuffed into lengths of French stick, blueberry muffins, orange and a cup of scalding tea. They looked out over the rain-sodden land. She had wanted to see the view but the cloud hung low and as they travelled north visibility worsened and the weather closed in, totally obscuring the vastness of the great heaving land. There were freckles of rain in the wind, striking the window with splinters of water that gradually accumulated into horizontal wavy bands that moved up and down with the motion of the train. In the foreground massive lumps of rock, shiny with rain protruded from the ground. Sheep ambled. Youthful streams and fast flowing rivers gushed over boulders, carving their way between fields. In the Borders, the spitting rain gave way to snow, obliterated the view. Drifting, it ledged on the sheep's fleecy backs. The journey was effortless. The heat blasting from the grill running through the carriage sapped and sedated the passengers. Her son dozed beside her.

Unfolding the map they got their bearings and headed east along the river then through a rather abandoned part of the city to the Necropolis. The macabre image of the Victorian cemetery had been firmly imprinted in her mind from watching the original Taggart series on television. The forest of sarcophagi, obelisks and the mausoleums crowded together overlooking the sprawling city was captivating. They walked around the cinder paths, reading and scanning as they passed the wealth and grandeur of a by-gone age. Peering over the map again they made for Merchant Square for lunch. Eating in true Scottish style, they had haggis fritters and Shetland mussels. With constant use the map was becoming limp with rain, gradually disintegrating into papier-mâché. In the Gallery of Modern Art nearby, they enjoyed an entertaining half-hour video of movement and motion; they saw bronze ice cream scoops, blank cheques, a wheel of heeled shoes and a hall of mirrors inside the entrance.

Outside it was still raining. The raw wet day was etched on people's faces. Ground down, they were hardened to the realities thrust on their city over the years. The dour harshness showed, scurrying out of the cold, the wind and the rain. Yet it was a proud city, the buildings grand, built to last, a wide paved openness, what you see is what you get. It was such a contrast to shopping at home, the smug warmth of the covered malls, door-to-door, no need to get wet and cold. Unlike the Glaswegians, they hadn't weathered. Nothing compared to the ferocious weather north of the border. They were wimps, especially the children, brought-up cushioned against reality. It lived-up to its 'No mean city' image.

Finishing at the Gallery sooner than expected there was time to walk along the Clyde. They followed the river off the map towards the sea. The placid grey slip had lost its heart. Unlike the bustle on the Thames, the Clyde was lifeless and eerily quiet. Apart from a swooping gull and the steady dimpling rain nothing broke the surface, no chugging engines, no churning propellers, no oar or swish of sail, no warning horns and calling out. Traffic fed across the many arteries spanning the river, allowing the Nesbitt family a glimpse of the smart glittering shops. Instead of jetties, boat yards, sheds, boats moored and cables and anchors and ropes lashed, modern buildings of steel and glass rose from its banks. Near the estuary in the murky distance there was a huddle of cranes. She took a photo and one close-up of she assumed a monumental crane, one to remind future generations of the prosperity that there had once been.

They sat in The Goose, overlooking Union Street hugging a Guinness. The smell of un-cleared plates lingered, behind them, the general clattering throng of a full bar. Glad to have seats they watched the steady stream of buses hissing passed. The passengers wiped the steamed-up windows with their sleeves and stared back out onto the pavement. With an urgent need of a cigarette people spilled outside The Goose, hopping from one leg to the other in the cold mingling with people who walked by with bags of shopping or their phones clamped to their ears, their umbrellas leaning against the rain. Water trickled continually in the gutter. It was grey and dismal. Boarding the train they removed their wet hats and jackets, pushed them onto the overhead rack and took a seat. Languishing in the extra space they dissolved into the welcoming warmth. Insulated from the sounds of the station the train quietly slipped away from the platform. The evening closed in around them. When they looked out again the darkness reflected their faces.

Her husband had been in the cupboard that housed the photos taken regularly until digital images became the norm. On the top of the pile was a picture of her as a teenager, tanned and raw-boned, wearing a bikini that she remembered painstakingly making, using a bra and briefs as templates. She was sitting on the beach in San Sebastian eating from a large bag of crisps. Even now she can remember the distinctive taste of the oil. It horrifies her to see herself self-harming. She wouldn't do that now any more than she would eat her way through a bar of chocolate or a packet of biscuits, claiming that she had just cleaned her teeth or bits would get caught in her teeth and rot her teeth. The consequences of consuming 'controlled' foods resulted in overwhelming guilt. And she knew the calorie value to be high and that the salt, sugar and fat were way beyond requirements and that there were no nutritional benefits in these forbidden foods and tempting though they may be she had become hard-wired over the years to resist.

'Dinner at 4 on Sunday. Nothing posh. Love from Mum x.' In reply to her email, they all accepted and came as though summoned. The reason for the impromptu meal was that the previous weekend each son had complained bitterly about not having anything in the fridge with which to make dinner and that they had to muster-up the energy to go and do some shopping, resulting in an omelette, a McDonalds and starvation, had she not donated half a chicken and saved the day. From then on she lost count of the number of meals she had prepared for the various combinations of her children and their partners. Most weekends the fridge was rammed with food and drink and by Sunday it was empty.

She felt below par. The prolonged winter was dragging its heels, she hadn't got a book on the go, she felt heavy, time was going by too quickly, she was itchy and achy and the bones of the book she was writing were all but done and she knew she would miss the pressure and it would leave a void.

The week ahead, however, proved busy, her friends were there lifting her out of her malaise. Every day was spoken for.

Driving back from her friend's house the petrol warning light suddenly lit up, distracting her like some horrible blemish. With one eye on its warm glow the petrol pump symbol clearly warned her that it was time to stop and get petrol and she took no comfort from the fact that her son had driven all the way from Amersham with the light on. The other eye was drawn to the black swarm of perfectly synchronised starlings dramatically sweeping along the by-pass, a shadow of swirling swooping choreography.

There was an email from her friend. It was time to meet up, to catch- up on the last few months since their last lunchtime soiree. It was arranged for the usual venue at the usual time. She had known Eileen for forty years. With a generous personality larger than life, she was like no other person. However big the room, her presence filled the space. It was an invitation to her husband's sixtieth birthday party that jolted their reunion. With their children grown-up there was time to get together again and so took to meeting up at the Swan.

For two days a week Eileen worked in a charity shop, where she was in her element, sifting and sorting the boxes and bags dumped by people like her. She was a shrewd bargain hunter, a risk taker, an Ebay addict, and loved nothing more than to make a killing. Even though she had no need for half the things she bought, she just could not resist the temptation. When they first met up she could not get over Eileen's collapsed face, but despite the turns of fate thrust upon her over the years, she hadn't changed, and at the smallest thing she roared with laughter, a wicked infectious laugh, throaty from too much smoking. Though now styled in a modern bob and tamed with hair straighteners, her once wild red hair was now *coloured* wild red, boasting that the dye cost a pound from the pound shop. It was typical Eileen.

She pulled into the car park and reversed into one of the many spaces. Always overestimating how long it took to drive the ten miles she was early as usual and sat for a moment in the car, listening to the radio, an easily forgettable farce, and tidying the pockets of accumulating parking tickets into a screwed-up ball of paper. It was undoubtedly a place for the older generation to meet. All the time cars pulled in depositing the grey and fragile. Dressed up and arms linked they tottered across the car park to make the most of the exclusive Golden Years Menu. Settling at a table to wait for Eileen she absently felt for her earrings. One was missing. No. They had been a special and expensive gift from a friend. Before going to the Swan she had been to the end of the garden, to the garage, posted a letter, and returned books to the library. It could be anywhere. Retracing her steps later, she started at the petrol pump, explaining briefly to the man filling his car her reason for scrutinizing the tarmac, then she walked as she had earlier, to the post box, examining the ground, then inside queuing up, all the time scanning the floor for the brown pearl. At the till they checked the lost property box and she left her name and contact details in case it turned up. Still scanning, she reluctantly returned to the car and there it was lying amongst the loose gravel.

Over and over in her mind she was deciding what to wear for the Private View of Fixations. Soon discarded clothes lay flung across the bed. In the end she chose the recent charity shop purchase in chocolate brown, thick tights and black wool jacket, a black/brown look. Taking another mirror she checked the back and the view from the side.

Waiting in the queue for her ticket had taken ages. When they reached the ticket windows two and four, the people being served before her seemed to want more than a ticket. One woman had found someone who listened to her and didn't want to let go. "Thank you my darlin'.", "Alright my love?" "You take care now my darlin', you take care now". Like a litany, for the whole station to hear, the irritating tropes and stock phrases went on and on in her cockney dialect, moving away then drawing back to the glass partition to thank him yet again. She lost count, and her patience, with the number of times the woman repeated herself, oblivious to the lengthening queue of agitated travellers. Trapped behind the glass, the ticket man smiled. What more could he could do? In her frustration she had resigned herself to catching the next train. Nevertheless she still made a dash to the waiting train on platform one, jumping on; it departed immediately. Daydreaming she looked out over the view she knew so well. It was drab.

Within an hour of leaving the station she was in Knightsbridge and on passing popped into Benetton, where two lovely little jumpers beckoned her back. She walked to the V&A and scrutinized the floor plan. It was too easy to amble about, to be saturated with seeing too much and concentrated instead on the great oak doors, the wrought iron, the ceramics, the furniture and the twentieth century exhibits. Seeing her Woolworth's plate made her smile. Needing tea she located the café sign and followed it. Picking up a floral tray she passed the counter displayed with scones, assorted muffins and hot-cross-buns, to beverages where she was passed a cup and saucer and her own pot of tea that she set down along with a tiny jug of milk. Carrying her tray she walked into a great airy room ornately pillared and tiled and filled with a comfortable muffled hum and the clink of afternoon tea. Although the big round tables could seat up to ten, people were afraid to intrude and invade, seeking instead their own island, including her. The tea quenched her parched throat. It warmed and relaxed and feeling restored again she walked to Prince Consort Road to meet up with her son. Anxious to be out of the cold wind they fell into The Queen's Arms for her son to have some much needed food. Being a haven for the 'after work' drink, the bar was soon filled to bursting. Their seats were hot and eagerly fell upon as soon as she shuffled and picked up her scarf. Bracing themselves, they descended into the underground at Gloucester Road. Being peak time it was understandably busy; they arrived at The Stone Space in Leytonstone sixteen stops later. The Private View was thronging, sipping wine, admiring, taking photos, smiling, acknowledging the effort. Her son and his contemporaries had hung their work the evening before on the plain white walls. It was impressive. At its height they said their goodbyes and slipped out to make their way back to Euston. The fast train was boarding. With moments to spare they ran to get it.

Reluctantly she pulled herself away from the fire. When deciding to go, she had not expected to be trudging through snow. Wrapping up she went out into the beastly weather to the spring concert in the church. Familiar faces were scattered amongst the pews. She looked at Peter in the next pew, like her he had been a 'Singers' member and like her he was singing Libera Me in his head. Once learnt, never forgotten. She was full of admiration for the soloists and the accompanists and she loved watching the interplay between them, the way they acknowledged their thanks to each other, a polite bow, an extended arm held aloft, smiling, a nod of the head. Like the Christmas concert it was well attended, especially considering the weather. At the Christmas concert audience participation had been programmed in. Sing-alongs and seasonal favourites had kept her alert and although she enjoyed singing, the rustle of standing up interrupted the flow of the evening. Singing the Holly and the Ivy she was reminded of being a choir-girl, shaking with nerves when it was her turn to sing a solo verse, the fear in her wobbly voice hard to control. And afterwards, the disappointment when she knew she hadn't sung well enough, how she knew she could sing.

Sunday 24th March. Despite the freezing temperatures and the continuing flurries, the paths and roads were free of snow and after an early dinner she went out. Apart from two dogs and the two men walking them Bury Field was desolate. The snow lifted and whipped against her umbrella. It had scoured and drifted in bands across the field and the mire underneath it was wetter than ever. Where for some reason they had escaped the covering of snow, the patches of grass were a disconcertingly glaringly emerald. Tears welled up and rolled over her cheeks, she could taste salt in the corners of her mouth. Now and then she pulled a tattered tissue from her pocket and mopped them up. The icy wind was vicious and too strong at times for the umbrella. Instead she pulled her hood up over her hat. She remembered a year ago, going to a work experience placement. At the entrance to the cow shed where the student was working the farmer stood in the warm spring sunshine, his hands in his overall pockets, complaining bitterly about the lack of rain and the fact that it was delaying the herd going out to pasture. It was hard to believe the weather could be so opposite. The brown whorls swirled into the graveyard and because of the flooding she returned home via the town.

Spring had paused. For more than a month winter's bone had not lessened. The inclement weather was there every day when she pulled back the curtains. The disagreeable stagnant cloud refused to budge and the moody sky dragged in flurries of snow on the merciless Arctic wind. Occupying her time and warming the kitchen, she launched into making hot-cross-buns and Easter treats decorated with mini-eggs. Not having been lavish about Easter, she felt that it was her contribution. She on the other hand had been treated to an impressive Easter egg, unexpectedly given by a friend who for years had felt sorry that she had never had one. It pleased him that he could bridge the gap and had presented her with one for many years, a habit that he found difficult to break. Once opened it didn't last long and the packaging soon stood in the corner like a Brabantia pedal bin.

As the cold wind funnelled along the track her hands were comforted by the warming cup of coffee she was holding. Placing the coffee on the fold down table she shed her coat and took a window seat. The train left late with an apology for the delay. Sipping it, she looked out over the threadbare downtrodden land, the shabby flattened verges of dry coarse grass, ivy hanging like bad hair, a tangle of briars lacing over the worn out grass with no hint of spring, the murky green canal threading its way between the fields that lay waiting for warmth, the lengthening days offering none. Frost lingered where the fretwork of branches cast shadows between the fields. A breath of cold air swept through the carriage when the train stopped and the doors opened, instantly dispersing the warm air that filtered through the grill by her feet. Going this way and that, planes ripped into the high blue sky and skeins of overhead cables strung out in silver lacy loops. On reaching Euston she had fallen into a dopy stupor. The train was full and people stood, somewhere behind her a child screeched. People were shuffling, reaching for their bags.

Taking the Northern Line she headed for the river. Crossing the road she stood taking in the view. Pulsating, churning water in its wake, the river bus had not long pulled away from its moorings, other cruise boats too were on the move, slowly and silently the London Eye rotated, buses filed across Westminster Bridge, everywhere there were visitors and tourists. Ahead, Big Ben read ten to eleven. Despite the sun it was bitterly cold and she was glad of her hat. Crossing Westminster Bridge, Big Ben struck eleven. People stopped in their tracks, they took photos, a father bent down towards his children and counted un, deux, trois. Taking the two flights of steps down, she walked along the South Bank towards the sea, past the lengthening queue for the newly located London Dungeon, the hub of people by the London Eye, past Jack Sparrow, past Darth Veda and the artists dressed in gold sprayed clothes, past the multi-cultural buskers all expecting to be rewarded for another cold day on the pavement. Gradually the people thinned out. The book stalls were setting up as were the many eateries, firing-up the ovens, the smell of tasty ethnic street food wafting. The tide was out, exposing slimy green stumps of rotting piles, oak groynes and jetties. Waves lapped and the gulls, geese and pigeons searched for food along the foreshore. In Tate Modern she made her way to the fourth floor, taking in the Red Flocked Wall, the Tumbling Felt, the Giant Lids, the Strip Lighting, the Galvanized Extraction, the Picassos and the Inner Space of Cubes, admiring, but not overly so, reading the blurb accompanying each piece. By twelve thirty, before it became hectic, she had ordered lunch. Although the restaurant was already humming the service was swift and she was soon outside again. While she had been inside, cloud had swept in and standing for a moment breathing in the smell of the sea she watched the boats and barges bobbing in the swell. From the South Bank she could see a flight of steps leading down to the beach and a couple of people beachcombing.

The thought excited her. To think that she could walk about where once people had stepped off a boat or gathered coal. Into her head rushed Mrs Lovatt's Pie Shop and Jack the Ripper and Oliver Twist and people pulling hand carts to the water's edge, she wildly pictured clippers and galleons, trading with far-away places, crossing continents, maps and stars everything that had gone before.

She had time and crossing the Millennium Bridge towards St Pauls she made for the narrow steps. Quickly she was gathering, absorbed, soaking up the history. Seeing her as a like-minded 'Mudlark' a woman approached. She had been collecting pieces of clay pipe, claiming that during the 16th century the disposable pipes were bought already filled with tobacco and then thrown away. Unlike the woman she didn't have a soft cotton bag in which to put her treasures and quickly her pockets were bulging and her bag wouldn't fasten. There were plenty of bones, worn smooth in the water, fragments of ceramics, lengths of clay pipes, a rusting iron tool and broken stoneware. Off the beaten track in the heart of London she was engrossed doing the most unlikely activity. It was bizarre. Beside her the shallow waves broke over the rocks and all around the backdrop of monumental buildings towered.

Leaving Victoria Embankment she cut through to the Strand and into Trafalgar Square, zigzagging to Piccadilly where, having time to spare before going into the Royal Academy she stopped for a coffee. The cleverness of the computer had printed a ticket for the Manet Exhibition called 'Portraying Life'. She liked to think that that was what she did in her writing, 'portraying life'. Murmuring echoed softly in the galleries. Manet's work depicted the advantages of his social class. She loved the fact that she could stand barely a breath away from his pictures, to see where his brushes stroked the canvas, where his hands lifted the work from the easel and did he ever envisage it so highly valued and admired, gathered together in one place. It was such a privilege. What a way to celebrate the last day of the first year of the rest of her life.

And so the first year of the rest of her life had come full circle. Already it was fizzing, frothing and foaming like the flourishing gauzy hedgerows bursting into life again. With everything to look forward to her zest for life had not subsided. Once again the dandelions took hold and the swallows returned.

EPILOGUE

For the whole of her first year of retirement he had been quietly simmering on the back-burner. The careless moment had changed Kristina's life forever. Shocked and upset she didn't want to have a baby and phoned her mother. "Poor Kristina, you have got to decide." And she did. Uncertainty was there all the way through. Everything petrified her. Where was she going to live? How was she going to manage? How could she afford a baby? What would her boyfriend say?

There was no going back. Since the summer he had anchored himself firmly. All through the Olympics, she had felt her body change, grappling to stay in control, swooning and grabbing out for something cool to hold on to. So the baby took shape, never giving a moment's peace. Elbows and knees kicked. She worked. All day or night she was on her feet and her job as a carer required lifting and tolerance. At times she had neither and lost her temper. At times she cried simply because she couldn't cope with everything, her increasing girth, the dragging heaviness, the tiredness, the backache, the heartburn, the constant nagging worry. It was depressing.

By the autumn the mound appeared, no more than a little hillock, pushing against her firm white skin and with it the deep-rooted apprehension began to melt. She was always hungry and ate everything, her speciality being pickled onions. In felt-tip pen she drew a big smiley face on her belly. The sense of insecurity and doubt returned at anti-natal classes, sometimes attending on her own, the other couples, mainly in their late twenties, made her feel uncomfortable. Their smug sideways looks, their cruel sly glances made her feel ashamed. Still there was stigma attached to a relatively young seemingly single mum-to-be. It had taken the whole nine months to come to terms with her fears and in the end she was calm. Her wide winning smile brought promise.

Arriving home, however, tired and stressed from the longer than expected stay in ward 9, she felt overwhelmed. The labour had been intense and nursing care sparse. Anxiety and the fears of not coping returned. With feelings fragile and finely balanced, convincing her otherwise would take time. No amount of advice could have prepared her for the emotional upheaval.

On April 3rd she was woken by her husband's phone, vibrating on the cupboard by the bed. He slept on.

At 10.36am she emailed her son.

Thinking of you.
With love to you and Kristina.
Mum x

Later, she sent another.

How's the little family doing?
Love from mum x

Isaac slithered into the world on the 3rd of April. In his diary where her husband wrote daily about crop rotation and the weather, he wrote 'love it'. He ached to see him, to take his finger over his downy cheek and brush of hair, to take his tiny hand, to feel him, to smell him, but he had to make do with photos sent via email and printed out on A4 paper. Madly he sat the pictures beside him on the settee to watch the football on Super Sunday. At last they met. Her husband gently cradled his grandson in his lumbering arms.

She had a great aversion to being called traditional names. She rather liked Baba-ghanoush or something African or Arabic or foreign. Until Isaac started speaking her Christian name would have to suffice. In the mean-time he communicated with laughing eyes, heart-melting gummy smiles and gentle sea-gull sounds.

May 1st 2013 Wednesday. It was the culmination of years of hard work. Her son had completed his PhD and reached the rarefied heights of academia. The wonderful achievement was to be celebrated at the graduation ceremony in the splendour of the Royal Albert Hall. For months she had been thinking about what she would wear, the weather ultimately being the deciding factor. Whittling the choice down to two outfits she gathered the accessories and tried them on, checking the views in the mirror from various stances. The evening before she traipsed downstairs to show her husband and get his opinion and approval. He barely glanced from the television, but chose the floaty green skirt and top instead of the dress. He did not stop to consider how she felt wearing either, the youth of the short figure-hugging rosy dress or what she considered as being the dowdy length of the skirt.

There was no doubt that she liked the outfit and the colour, but she pictured herself wearing it and thought about what she would say at seeing herself in it. Only the other day she had been critical of a woman wearing a similar length skirt and she had thought at the time, how old fashioned, all that fabric wrapping round her legs as she walked. It made her look frumpy and older than her years, wearing it because it was a good, serviceable skirt, too good to throw away. The charity shops were full of good clothes, bought when they were fashionably long or fashionably loose. She did not mind wearing clothes coveted from the charity shops. When she was at school the pupils were taken aback if she told them where she had made a purchase, they thought it was skanky to even frequent them. Sometimes she said it to get their reaction.

The next morning she showered and dressed and went downstairs, unnecessarily moving a plate from the dining room, where her husband was watching the news, to the dishwasher, only to turn round, walk back upstairs and change into the dress.

It could not have been a more gloriously warm spring day and the dress was perfect.

The well-planned itinerary moved effortlessly, the taxi, the train, the underground, the lunch, the photos taken on the steps, along with hundreds of other proud parents and friends, and finally, at five, seating for the ceremony. Below, the undergraduates mingled in gowned excitement. With the fanfare, the pageantry began with the dignitaries processing in, many wearing their academic dress, with vibrant gowns and hoods and hats to take their places on the stage followed by the Imperial mace. After a brief address the graduands filed from their seats and across the stage in an orderly procession where their names were read out and their photos taken. Clapping broke out when there was an extra-special award. The special day ended all too soon with a champagne reception, held, funnily enough, where she had been many times for British Nutrition Foundation meetings.

There was an email. Her latest book 'Between the Stars' was in its final stages of production. And the production coordinator asked her to check the manuscript and to make amendments where necessary. A large glass of velvety Spanish wine helped her to focus. Her third book; she could hardly contain herself, the cover 'Deep inside the Milky Way' a NASA image, so hauntingly beautiful, and she remembered the email 'Have an outstanding day.'